MW00488713

Hartmut Eberlein

Around
Mont Blanc

The finest valley and mountain walks
50 selected mountain walks around Mont Blanc

With 54 colour photographs,
49 1:50.000 walking maps
and a 1:460.000 overview map

ROTHER · MUNICH

Front cover (Michael Waeber):
A monarch and its satellites: View over the Lac Blanc and the Lac Blanc
Hut (meanwhile destroyed by an avalanche) to Mont Blanc.

Frontispiece (photo on page 2):
Fairy-tale meadow below Mont Blanc.

All photographs by the author, with the exception of the photos on
pages 34 (Karsten Ewald), 17, 21, 29, 33, 43, 53, 58, 61, 67, 79, 83, 85,
87, 89, 94/95, 107, 109 (Walter Hellberg), 57, 65, 73, 115 (François
Labande), 41, 48, 63, 70, 75, 77, 97, 98, 100, 102, 105 (Martin
Ottersbach)

Cartography: Maps 1:50.000
© ign (Institut Géographique National), Paris (Autorisation N° 90 1068)

Translation: Tony Pearson

1st edition 2000
© Bergverlag Rother GmbH, München

ISBN 3-7633-4804-2

Distributed in Great Britain by Cordee, 3a De Montfort Street, Leicester
Great Britain LE1 7HD, www.cordee.co.uk
in USA by AlpenBooks, 3616 South Road, C-1, Mukilteo,
WA 98275 USA, www.alpenbooks.com

ROTHER WALKING GUIDES

Crete West · Iceland · La Palma · Mallorca · Mont Blanc · Norway South · Provence · Sardinia ·
Valais East · Around the Zugspitze

**Dear mountain lovers! We would be happy to hear your opinion and
suggestions for amendment to this Rother walking guide.**

BERGVERLAG ROTHER · Munich
**D-85521 Ottobrunn · Haidgraben 3 · Tel. 0049/89/608669-0, Fax -69
Internet** http://www.rother.de · **E-mail** bergverlag@rother.de

Preface

The name Mont Blanc conjures up a picture of steep, fissured glaciers, giddy rock pinnacles and mighty ice faces. And yet, by far the greater number of visitors to the area who are involved in mountaineering, at whatever level that may be, are actually mountain walkers. Through their proximity to the glaciers, and because of their relatively modest height, in contrast to the mountains which they allow to be observed, the walks in the mountains of the Mont Blanc Massif offer the most varied views and plenty of rest places. Sometimes the paths described lead directly past rock and ice, but always with the necessary distance required by the cautious, not too-daring walker.

On the other hand, walking in the Mont Blanc area signifies more than walking in the lower alpine areas. The highest objectives in such areas are here the parameters within which the walks take place, and a good few of the walks involve ascents of 1000 metres or even more. Moreover, this means that, at least in July, and particularly after winters with plenty of snow, you should carry an ice-axe, or at any rate telescopic trekking poles, which will often prove very useful.

Many of the walks described here have been undertaken by the author with his very young children. Indeed *all* of the walks described here can be done »en famille«, if necessary by tying on to a short rope, although plenty of rest stops and a penchant for story telling are important too. It is really only in the case of the Tour of Mont Blanc that too high a demand should not be made, for when it is absolutely necessary to reach the hut which is the day's objective, the element of fun could be lost.

As far as circumstances permit, cable lifts and funicular railways have been included in the itineraries, especially in the case of descents. Walking downhill, normally so popular in other areas, is less to be recommended here in view of the generally very steep paths.

The region around Mont Blanc is in many cases not an isolated one. This, of course, is the case for the walks too, and in particular for the classical Tour of Mont Blanc (TMB). Nevertheless, a good number of the walks described are relatively quiet.

And so dear reader, walk in the Mont Blanc Massif, discover one of the most beautiful high mountain areas in the world from closest proximity, sometimes with a slight shudder, but also with a sense of spontaneous joy at the mighty beauties which are offered to you.

Hartmut Eberlein

Contents

Tourist Information

Structure of the guide
The contents give an overview of all the walks described. For each of the suggested walks there is an initial summary of the important information. Following on from this is a thorough appreciation of the walk and then a short description of it. The text is completed with a coloured walking map showing the route and a colour photograph. An important component of the guide is the index at the end, in which all the mentioned valleys, mountain groups, valley bases, starting points and walking objectives are listed. Finally, a map provides an overview of where the various walks are within the Mont Blanc Massif.

Grade
The walks described in this guide are generally easy and can be done in stout shoes and without any training. Sure-footedness and a head for heights are however necessary for most of the routes. So that the demands of individual routes can be better estimated, the numbers of the suggested walks have been colour coded. The colours are to be interpreted as follows:

Early summer in the mountains.

The Chamonix valley.

BLUE
These paths are perfectly waymarked, sufficiently wide and only slightly steep, and therefore also relatively safe even in poor weather. Children and elderly people can do these walks without any great danger.

RED
These walks are adequately waymarked, but on the whole the paths are narrow and there are short sections which are somewhat exposed. Short stretches of these walks may be protected by steel cables, and therefore the walks should only be undertaken by mountain walkers who are sure-footed and properly equipped.

BLACK
These walks are also adequately waymarked, but the paths are narrow and there are longer steep sections. In places they can be very exposed and sometimes they will require the use of the hands. This means that these walks should only to be done by experienced mountain walkers who are absolutely sure-footed and well trained.

Waymarks

In addition to continual waymarks indicating the path, there are also numerous signs. Route finding is therefore made significantly easier. For those who are not familiar with the area a compass is a useful help in orientation.

Dangers

Although the walks described here almost exclusively follow well-trodden paths, caution is required at the occasional points where a slip is possible, such as when crossing steep slopes or in areas threatened by rockfall. This particularly applies to the crossing of snow-filled gullies or steep snowfields. Summer thunderstorms can also be as source of danger.

Equipment

Stout walking shoes with a good tread, adequate clothing, plus a rucksack with a pullover, waterproofs, anorak and some provisions (water bottle!) are a requirement. Climbing equipment is not necessary.

Maps

The coloured walking maps included with each of the suggested walks are an essential part of the guide. However, this does not make other maps redundant. A basic requirement is the 1:50 000 ign-Map »Mont Blanc« but better still are the 1:25 000 ign 3531 ET and 3630 OT maps. With the help of these maps and the recommended compass it is also not too difficult to identify the mountains one is gazing at.

Walking times

The times given are generous, but are however, *pure* walking times. As a rule uphill, downhill and total times are mentioned. For circuits or longer tours the times for the different stages of the walk are given.

Best time of year

The recommended best time of year takes into consideration snow-free periods, the times when cable cars are running, guest houses open etc. Mention is also made of especially beautiful or suitable months for walking. As numerous overnight stops are required on the Tour of Mont Blanc it is necessary to point out the frequent problem of the overfilled accommodation. As the high season in France clearly peaks around the middle of August, it is recommended not to undertake the Tour until the latter part of August. But, already by the beginning of September support from the public transport system starts to decline. Whoever still wants to walk at the end of September would do well to check out the situation, i.e. opening times, etcetera.

Companions.

Ascent
This refers to the difference in height between the lowest and highest point of a walk. In case of doubt the direction (up or down) is separately noted.

Huts
In the section on »Food/Accommodation« all of the bases which are open in summer on a particular walk are indicated.

Mechanical aids for ascent

Often walks are started or ended from points which can be reached by cable cars or chair lifts. One should be aware that these are frequently only open in the summer months of July, August and September. At other times of the year it is often only possible to reach these points on foot.

Special Information about the Area

Tourist information centres can be found in the larger valley bases and through these it is possible to book accommodation etc from home, i.e. through addresses which can be obtained.

For alpine information the Office de la Haute Montagne Gerard Devouassoux (OHM) in Place de l'Eglise in Chamonix is the pertinent organisation. From this office it is possible to get all the up-to-date information about the conditions in the mountains (Tel. 50-53-22-08). The daily weather reports »Meteo« are hung up here three times a day.

In addition the weather forecast is also displayed on the little information kiosk of the Tourist Information Office in Argentière. The weather report can also be obtained by telephone from abroad: Tel. 0033-50-53-03-40. The automatic telephone forecast is, of course, only in French. In the office (OHM) one can manage reasonably well with English. A similar service is available in Italy in Courmayeur at the Office du Val Veni, Tel. 0165-84-10-21. Other telephone numbers:

Tourist Office Chamonix (Office du tourisme de Chamonix)Tel. 50-53 00 24
Tourist Office Courmayeur Tel. 0165-84 20 60

In emergency the numbers for the rescue services are:

France: Peloten de Gendarmerie de Haute Montagne (PGHM)
Chamonix, Tel. 50-53 16 89
St. Gervais Tel. 50-78 1081
From Switzerland or Italy the dialling code is 0033

Italy: Guides bureau Tel. 0165 –84 42 35
Poste de Secours de Courmayeur Tel.0165-84 42 35
From France the dialling code is 0039

Switzerland: Poste de la police cantonale du Valais Tel. 027-117
Gendarmerie in Orsières Tel. 027-4 11 06
Dialling code from France: 0041

Valleys and Valley Bases

FRANCE

Chamonix, which is in the wide Arve valley, is at a height of 1040m and is best described as a »mountain town«: the centre of alpinism in the Mont Blanc range. There are all possible standards of accommodation, which are almost sufficient for the number of visitors: for addresses etc see the introductory section. All possible types of shops and amenities can be found (swimming pools, hospital, cinema, tennis courts etc.).

The much smaller town of **Argentière**, 8km up the valley from Chamonix, is particularly crowded with visitors in winter. In summer there is rather less hustle and bustle than in Chamonix. There are equally good shopping facilities. The structure of the old town centre in Argentière is still well preserved.

The last village in the upper Arve valley, **le Tour**, can be reached on foot along a road from the railway station in Montroc in 15 min. Some small shops and hotels are found in Le Tour. There is a cable car to Col de Balme.

Vallorcine is a railway station on the Chamonix-Martigny railway and the main place in this somewhat quieter valley. There are satisfactory shopping facilities.

Les Houches is about 8kms up the valley from Chamonix. A rather spread out village with bus connections and adequate shopping.

The smaller village of **les Contamines** is 8kms from St. Gervais in the Val Montjoie. Sufficient shops. Somewhat above the town (3kms away) is the end of the road at Notre Dame de la Gorge: a good snack bar.

ITALY

Courmayeur is the largest valley base on the Italian side. A relatively long way from the actual mountaineering, the view from Courmayeur with its elevation of Mont Blanc is especially impressive. All necessary facilities are available.

The road leads through the **Val Ferret** via Planpincieux, 1564m and La Vachey, 1642m, to Arnuva, 1769m. There are no shopping facilities in the valley. In summer there is a bus service.

The **Val Veni** is the most beautiful of the Italian Mont Blanc valleys. Camping available with superb views of the mountains immediately above. Practically no shopping facilities. Very heavily visited during good weather in summer (big parking problem; buses best used).

SWITZERLAND

Champex is a very beautifully situated holiday village on a mountain lake worth seeing. Campsite, youth hostel, holiday flats and hotels. A place particularly suited to mountaineers, which in comparison to the Chamonix valley is very quiet.

A small road leads into the **Swiss Val Ferret** from Orsières. Praz de Fort, 1151m, La Fouly, 1592m and Ferret, 1700m are the starting points for going up to the huts. Apart from Ferret, a small village organised for summer tourism, La Fouly is the most inviting place in the valley with a particularly nice campsite. The post bus travels from Orsières to Ferret. The road ends about 1km from Ferret at 1775m.

Abbreviations

E	East
GR	Grande Route (long-distance footpath)
Hr	hour/s
IGN	Institut geographique national
Min	minute/s
N	North
S	South
TMB	Tour of Mont Blanc
W	West

Some French Alpine Terms

Aiguille	rock pinnacle	Neige	snow
Averses	precipitation	Névé	hard snow crust
Bréche	gap	Orage	thunderstorm
Bussole	compass	Piolet	iceaxe
Chemin	path	Refuge	mountain hut
Chute de Pierre	stonefall	Selle	saddle
Chute de serac	falling ice	Télépherique	cable car
Eau potable	drinking water	Télésiege	chair lift

The contrast can hardly be greater: a display of flowers and glacial mountains.

1 Tête de Balme, 2321m

Small viewpoint above the Col de Balme

Col de Balme cable car station – Col de Balme – Tête de Balme

Location: Le Tour, 1453m
Starting point: Car park of Le Tour- Charamillon – Col de Balme cable car
Food/Accommodation: Refuge du Col de Balme (20 beds), 2191m.
Walking time: Ascent 40 min; Descent 25 min.
Grade: Easy walking.
Highest point: 2321m (summit).
Ascent: 160m.
Best time of year: July to September.
Advice: It is better to start the walk at the intermediate cable car station (Charamillon) which requires an extra 1¼ hrs. From there follow the marked path (TMB) to the Col de Balme.
Map: ign 3630.

This walk provides a particularly fine view of Mont Blanc and the Chamonix Aiguilles in front of it. The modest hospitality at the Col de Balme becomes more welcome after two further excursions in the area. On the Swiss side of the Col de Balme a very nice snowfield is to be found up to the middle of summer where glissading can be practised with little danger. Children in particular will enjoy this. On the French side, an almost level walk leads to the Lac de Charamillon, a small lake cut off by a moraine.

From the **Col de Balme cable car station** follow the path almost horizontally northwards to the Col de Balme. Go past the small inn and up with little exertion towards the northwest, more or less following the edge of the ridge to reach the summit of the **Tête de Balme**. The descent to the Col de Balme takes the same path.

Descent: The descent from the Col de Balme can be done either direct to the cable car station or via the **Col des Posettes**. In order to do the latter, it is best to follow the path which begins a little above the hut and leads WNW (a

Below the Col de Balme.

variant on the TMB) from which one can descend directly to the Col des Posettes in about 20 min. From the Col des Posettes itself a wide path leads back to the intermediate station, Charamillon, from where one is best off sparing the knees by gliding down in the cable car. About ¾ hr should be allowed for this little detour.

2 Aiguillette des Posettes, 2201m

Mountain ridge with fine views above the alpine meadows of the Arve Valley

Tré le Champ – Aig. des Posettes – Col des Posettes – Col de Balme cable car station

Location: Argentière, 1244m and le Tour.
Starting point: Tré le Champ car park. As the round trip ends in le Tour, it is advisable to take a bus to Tré le Champ at the start of the walk and from le Tour to Argentière at the end of the walk.
Food/Accommodation: Refuge du Col de Balme, 2191m.
Walking time: Ascent to Aig. des Posettes 2½ hrs. From there 1½ hrs to Col de Balme. From here just a few minutes to the summit station of Col de Balme, 2162m.
Grade: Easy walking.
Highest point: 2201m (summit).
Ascent: 1080m.
Best time of year: July to September.
Advice: From Col de Balme the walk can be significantly shortened, by taking the wide path to the Charamillon intermediate station. The walk is not as worthwhile in the reverse direction.
Map: ign 3630.

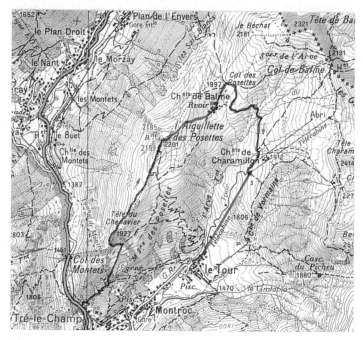

The Alpine Meadow huts of Chalet de Balme.

The walk over the ridge of the Aiguilette des Posettes begins with quite a steep path, luckily in the shade of a dense mountain forest. Once most of the height gain has been made, the forest is left, the other ridge side is taken and one has a broad view of the mountains of the massif. A small summit invites a rest, from where the main summit can be admired in peace. If it is too windy one can descend to the Chalet de Balme to rest.

In **Tré le Champ** the ascent starts a few metres above the town at a car park. First of all follow a path through the thick mountain forest past **Chalet Chaleyre**. At a fork in the path continue upwards to the left to a second fork above the edge of the forest. Now continue left, crossing the large mountain ridge of the Aiguilette des Posettes, which is then followed to the **summit**. On the other side the path soon leaves the ridge and goes down towards the right to the huts in the Alpine meadows of the **Chalet de Balme**. Now it continues almost level to the **Col des Posettes**. From here, walk on the slightly rising path to the **Col de Balme**. After this section of the walk, which is particularly strenuous on hot days, the modest hospitality at the Col de Balme is welcome, before a few minutes' walk leads to the cable car station and you are whisked down to the valley.

3 Refuge Albert I., 2702m

Large mountaineering hut under the Aiguille du Chardonnet

From the Col de Balme (cable car) to the hut and back

Location: le Tour and Argentière, 1244m.
Starting point: Cable car car park Le Tour – Charamillon – Col de Balme.
Food/Accommodation: At the end of the walk.
Walking time: Ascent 2½ hrs; Descent 1½ hrs.
Grade: Easy walk with some exposed sections.

Highest point: 2702m.
Ascent: 550m.
Best time of year: August
Advice: Some of the exposed sections are protected. The last 100 metres to the hut are generally covered in snow.
Map: ign 3630.

The large hut, which is named after the mountaineering Belgian King, Albert I, is a very much visited hut. From here, the mountaineer who is experienced at glacier walking can cross the Col du Tour to the Cabane de Trient, and one sees many alpinists starting off to the Aiguille du Tour and the Aiguille du Chardonnet (little thistle peak). The superb views of the Glacier du Tour and the Aiguille du Chardonnet, however, make the efforts of those only visiting the hut very worthwhile.

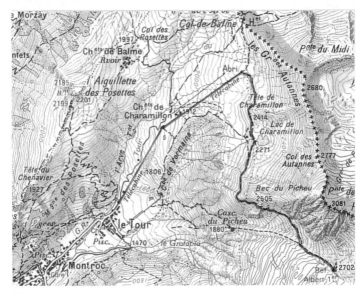

From the **Col de Balme cable car station** continue in a southerly direction. The path to the hut continues on the flat next to the **Lac de Charamillon**. It is only after the path turns to the west and above the snout of the **Glacier du Tour** that it becomes somewhat exposed in places and demands concentration in walking. After some rather airy passages where some ancient metal rails can be admired, the path traverses steeply upwards over the crest of the moraine. Because of the proximity of the glacier there is a snowfield on the left-hand side of the ascent path until late in the summer, which, with suitable practice, can be used for »glissading« in descent. Just below the **hut**, there is another short steep section but there is almost always a safe and easily-negotiated track. The **descent** follows the same path. It is important to make sure that the moraine is not followed too far downwards, or one misses the rightward fork to the cable car station. The direct route to the valley via Casc. du Picheu is not to be recommended for the mountain walker.

Aiguille du Chardonnet from the path to the Refuge Albert I.

4 Glacier d'Argentière, P. 1574m

Up to the viewpoint above the village and glacier of Argentière

From Le Tour to P. 1574 and back to Argentière

Location: Argentière, 1244m.
Starting point: Le Tour car park. As the walk finishes in Argentière, it is sensible to take the bus from there to Le Tour.
Food/Accommodation: None.
Walking time: In ascent: 1½ hrs; in descent to Argentière: ½ hr.
Grade: Easy walking.
Highest point: 1608m.

Ascent: About 250m in total.
Best time of year: July to September.
Advice: From P. 1574m. it is possible to follow the path on the right hand bank (NE) of the Glacier d'Argentière. However, under no circumstances should one attempt to descend directly on the side of the glacier.
Map: ign 3630.

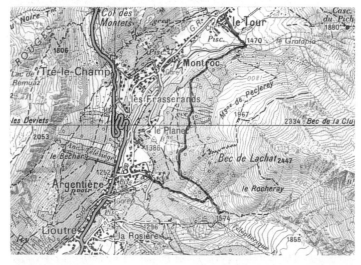

The relatively short walk to the so-called »Pierre à Bosson« is always likely to be a fairly quiet one. When one then stands underneath the great icefall of the Argentière Glacier to enjoy a hardly-deserved rest, it is also possible to get a view into the mysterious-looking »Valley of the North faces« above the Argentière Glacier. Hopefully one dreams then of visiting this fascinating glacial valley on a future walking trip. However, high alpine experience is required for this.

Le Tour with Aig. Rouges.

From **Le Tour** take a wide path from the southeast edge of the village in the same direction until at about 1470m the glacial streams of the Glacier du Tour can be crossed by means of several bridges. Now it is necessary to follow the slightly rising path (*Petit Balcon Nord*). About 20 minutes after the bridge the path forks: go up to the left. The path then continues, alternately up and then down, above the village of Argentière going upwards to the northeast in the direction of a prominent moraine ridge. At a suitable point with a beautiful view over the glacier one should choose a place to have a rest and eventually turn back.

The **descent** goes back via the ascent path until above Argentière. Now leave the familiar path and go left where after several zigzags you will arrive in the unspoilt old part of Argentière.

5 Refuge de Loriaz, 2020m

Varied walking day above Vallorcine

Vallorcine – Barberine Waterfall – Emosson Reservoir – Refuge de Loriaz – Courteray

High route to the Refuge de Loriaz.

Location: Vallorcine, 1260m, situated on the far side of the Col des Montets.
Starting point: On the outskirts of the village of Vallorcine at le Molard, 1210m: parking.
Food/Accommodation: Refuge de Loriaz. On the other side of the reservoir, which is in Switzerland, there is a snack bar.
Walking time: Ascent: 4½ hrs; Descent to Couteray: 1½ hrs.
Grade: The walk is easy but long and in the sun.
Highest point: 2075m.
Ascent: Nearly 1000m.
Best time of year: July/August.
Advice: From the Refuge de Loriaz it is best to take the wide path down to Couteray. The shorter path direct via Siseray is less pleasant in descent.
Map: ign 3630.

The high path from Lac d'Emosson to the Chalet de Loriaz offers an interesting day's walk in a rather more isolated area of the Mont Blanc massif. In view of the open, sun-exposed situation an early start is recommended. From the le Molard part of **Vallorcine** go up a slightly-rising path in a northerly direction. After about half an hour the **Barberine** Waterfall is reached. It is worth spending a while here before continuing along the steep path to the artificial lake. From the level of the **dam wall** it is possible to cross over this onto the Swiss side to a small guesthouse (overnight stay possible). Back again on the French side, walk along an almost even path in a southerly direction to the **Chalet de Loriaz**.

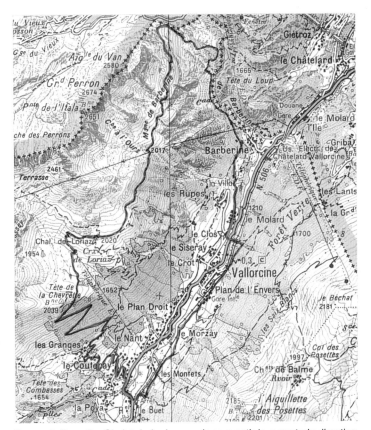

Descent: From the Chalet de Loriaz go along a path in a westerly direction until after a few minutes, beyond the first bend in the path, a wide path is reached which can be comfortably descended to the le Couteray district of Vallorcine. On arriving in the valley about half an hour is needed to walk down the valley to le Molard, the starting point. If enough time is left, it is recommended not to follow the road but rather to take a path on the true right hand side of the valley stream and the right of the railway until at the height of the railway station in Vallorcine before going back along the path to Molard.

6 Refuge de la Pierre à Bérard, 1924m

Walk below Mont Buet

Le Buet railway station - Refuge de la Pierre à Bérard and back

Location: Vallorcine, 1260m.
Starting point: At the small railway station in le Buet, parking.
Food/Accommodation: Refuge de la Pierre à Bérard (30 places), 1924m.
Walking time: Ascent: 2 hrs; Descent: 1¼ hrs.
Grade: Easy walking.
Highest point: 1924m.
Ascent: 600m.

Best time of year: July to about mid-September.
Advice: Experienced mountain walkers can climb to the summit of Mont Buet from the hut in about 4 hrs. This generally popular ascent leads at times over snowfields so that suitable equipment is needed. The path can clearly be followed from the indication on the IGN map.
Map: ign 3630.

The walk to the Refuge de la Pierre à Bérard leads one into a less spectacular corner of the Mont Blanc Massif. Despite the relatively deeply cut valley the surrounding mountains do not look so unapproachable. Consequently this half-day excursion takes on a very friendly character while the waterfall at the beginning also offers a spectacular viewpoint.

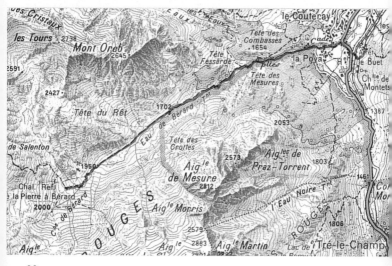

At the starting point, le Buet.

From the **le Buet railway station** follow a well signposted path to the waterfall. Continue upwards on the true right bank of the stream in the valley which leads to the **Refuge de la Pierre à Bérard**. The path follows the bottom of the valley, at times a little monotonous, but the vegetation and the ever-changing perspective on the Aiguilles Rouges ensure that the hour in the valley is quickly over. If you are walking with children, there are, especially in the upper part of the valley, several good play areas by the stream. However, bear in mind that a fast-flowing stream does present a continual source of danger.

Descent: The return path through the mountain valley is quickly over. It is recommended at the split in the path where it goes off right to the waterfall to go left over the bridge and to return to le Buet via le Couteray. In doing so one sees the waterfall from both sides and gets to know the hamlet of le Couteray. However care is required in crossing the N 506, particularly at the bridge over the valley stream!

7 Lac Blanc, 2352m

The ice lake in the Chamonix Aiguilles Rouges

Flegère cable car station – Lac Blanc – Cable car station

Location: Chamonix, Argentière.
Starting point: Chamonix les Praz; Flegère cable car station. Parking.
Food/Accommodation: Modest mountain hut at Lac Blanc.

Walking time: 1¾ hrs in ascent; ¾ hr in descent.
Grade: Unproblematic mountain walking. Relatively steep last section before the hut.
Highest point: Lac Blanc, 2352m.
Ascent: 630m, including the ascent involved on the path back.
Best time of year: July to mid Sept.
Advice: In some years the lake is largely frozen over until the middle of August. Don't go on the ice!
Map: ign 3630.

The walk from the midway station of the Flegère-Index cable car is among the most frequently walked, indeed sometimes overcrowded walks in the Chamonix Aiguilles Rouges. But this is doubtless justified, for the view of the Aiguille Verte, the Chamonix Aiguilles and Mont Blanc is among the finest views that the walker can be offered. Moreover, the Lac Blanc offers hospitality, and the very interesting ice lake is often frozen over even late in the year, only mirroring the Aiguilles Vertes in September or October.

From the **Flegère Midway Station** 1877m, first descend slightly in a northerly direction. Then take a wide path over the fairly ugly scree slope, which is taken by several lifts. This goes up somewhat leading past the small **Lac de la Flegère**, finally steepens and goes up through a small high valley to the plateau where a number of lakes are found. Not visible on the right-hand side are the Cheserys lakes and in front is the larger **Lac Blanc** with the Refuge du Lac Blanc. The path has a number of short cuts, which one should avoid under all circumstances. The frequent ascent of the main path and the many short cuts has already led to considerable erosion on the slopes. Discipline is required from mountain walkers to avoid any further damage.

In **descent** one generally follows the ascent path. As a variant one can spend a few minutes walking along the path towards the Chalet de Cheserys. This leads to the left below the hut. In doing so you get to the Grand Balcon Sud, which is followed in a south-westerly direction into the basin below the cable car. A short, somewhat unpleasant ascent back up, leads to the cable car station from where one can comfortably glide down to the valley.

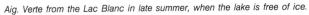

Aig. Verte from the Lac Blanc in late summer, when the lake is free of ice.

8   Lac Blanc, 2352m (via the Via Ferrata)

One of the few walks in the area with a via ferrata

Tré le Champ – Lac Blanc – Flegère

Location: Argentière, Chamonix.
Starting point: Tré le Champ or the car park somewhat below the Col des Montets, 1417m.
Food/Accommodation: Hut at the Lac Blanc.
Walking time: 3½ hrs to the Lac Blanc; ¾ hr from there to Flegère.
Grade: Generally easy mountain walking. The steep section, which is protected by

ladders and a steel cable, is more impressive than difficult. Nevertheless rope protection is needed for inexperienced and for children.
Highest point: 2352m.
Ascent: 1000m.
Best time of year: From July to about the middle of September.
Advice: Quite strenuous walk which is fully in the sun. Therefore, start early!
Map: ign 3630.

The ascent from the hamlet of Tré le Champ to Lac Blanc is one of the most worthwhile walks in the whole Mont Blanc Massif. However, due to the amount of ascent and the via ferrata, even if it is easy, this walk cannot be unreservedly recommended to all mountain walkers. From the path it is frequently possible to see climbers enjoying themselves in their airy pursuit on the sun-filled rock slabs above. This is particularly spectacular on the Aiguillette d'Argentère. This small peak is right next to the path. In the upper section, a beautiful, normally ice-free lake is passed, which is below the Refuge du Lac Blanc. The more daring can bathe here.

In **Tré le Champ** the path begins at the small car park just above the village on the left (western) side of the road. Take the path, which first ascends gradually until a fork is reached above an old, disused chair lift. Now continue upwards to the right until almost under the rock faces, also known as the Dalle de Remuaz. Without missing the path or stumbling over blocks by gazing in astonishment at the climbers you arrive almost at the foot of the small rock peak, the Aiguillette d'Argentière. Immediately behind this the fairly easy via ferratta begins, where it is necessary to ascend a number of iron ladders. Rope protection is, however, hardly necessary. Above a fork in the path is reached from where the route to the Lac Blanc is signposted. First stay to the right and then go along the hilly ground on the edge of the Cheserys lakes. From here it is only 20 minutes to the **hut**, which can only be seen at a very late stage.

Descent: The continuation of the path to the Flegère cable car station follows the path of Route 7 in the opposite direction.

The small via ferrata behind the Aig. d'Argentière.

9 Glacier d'Argentière, P. 2338m

A view into the chaos of the largest ice falls of the Glacier d'Argentière

Croix de Lognan – P. 2338m – Croix de Lognan

Location: Argentière, Chamonix.
Starting point: Argentière-Chosalets; Valley station of the Lognan – Grands Montets cable car. Carpark.
Food/Accommodation: Chalet de Lognan.
Walking time: 1¼ hrs ascent; ¾ hr descent.
Grade: Easy mountain walking.
Highest point: 2338m.

Ascent: 370m.
Best time of year: July and August.
Advice: The walk can also be finished at P. 2168m from where the view is already very good, but then you miss out on the experience of walking along the crest of the moraine.
Map: ign 3630.

The Mont Blanc Massif is distinguished by the fact that on the north side, i.e. in the Arve Valley, large glaciers descend to a relatively-low level. Therefore from a number of starting points it is possible via short walks to reach view points above the glacial tongues and to admire the varied glacial movements, shapes and dangers. This walk visits one of the best points for such observation.

From the midway station, the **Croix de Lognan**, 1973m of the Aiguilles de Grand Montets cable car first of all follow a farly ugly track in an easterly direction. Above the **Chalet de Lognan** the path forks to the southeast and the **viewpoint** 2168m is soon reached. From here there is a marvellous view of the icefalls. It is, however, very worthwhile to continue up the moraines to gain a still better view and impression of the glacier and of the surroundings. As a rule the walk is finished at **Point 2338m**. The continuation of the walk

On the moraine of the Glacier d'Argentière.

goes for a short stretch over the glacier *with sections protected by ladders and chains* continuing to the highest rock island in the glacier from where one has to step onto the glacier. The further ascent above Point 2338m can, therefore, only be undertaken by suitably-experienced alpinists.

The **descent** from Point 2338m takes the ascent path. Descent via the Chalet Lognan and the ski slope is not at all to be recommended as this is a very rocky and unpleasant route.

10 Grand Balcon Sud

Walk over one of the great panoramic trails of the Arve Valley

Col des Montets – Flegère

The Grand Balcon.

Location: Chamonix and Argentière.
Starting point: Col des Montets car park, 1416m.
Food/Accommodation: Only at the destination, unless one goes via the huts at the Lac Blanc.
Walking time: 4 hrs.
Grade: Altogether an easy walk, but at times it traverses some steep slopes.

Highest point: 2110m.
Ascent: 700m.
Best time of year: July/August.
Advice: There are many possible variants on the recommended route, which could lead to mountain walkers losing their way. However, if the route of the TMB is followed there shouldn't be any unpleasant surprises.
Map: ign 3630.

The route from Col des Montets to Flegère is the somewhat more harmless variant to Walk 8. After admiring the garden of plants at Col des Montets the Grand Balcon is reached after a short ascent, from where a splendid view of the great mountains of the area can be enjoyed. The path, which is popular, is wide and easy to walk.

From **Col des Montets** go up the waymarked path in a generally westerly direction until a more or less wide band, or rather rock step in the Aiguilles Rouges, which is followed almost all the way to the **Flegère Cable car** station. It is very important to look out for the markings on this path, as in the second half there are any number of other paths branching off and it is easy to lose the proper path. Our route involves hardly any great gain in height

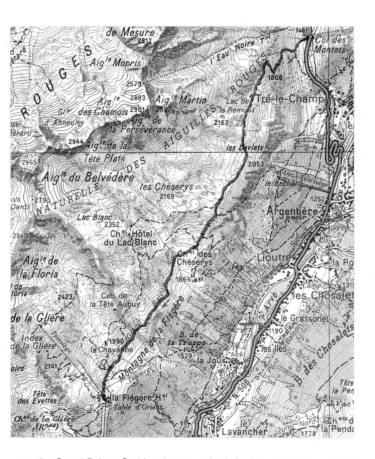

once the Grand Balcon Sud has been reached. As the route is exposed to the sun and there are no refreshment points en route it is strongly recommended to carry supplies of water.

The **descent** is via the cable car from Flegère to les Praz (see Walk 7). It is, of course, also possible to descend on foot, but in the upper section the path mainly follows the ski slopes and is therefore not very pleasant. Also in the lower section the path is not very worthwhile, so that the walk down to the valley is altogether not to be recommended.

11 Grand Balcon Nord

The somewhat cooler viewing terrace of Argentière

From Croix de Lognan to le Lavancher

Location: Argentière, 1224m.
Starting point: Valley station of the Argentière – Croix de Lognan – Aig. des Grandes Montets cable car.
Food/Accommodation: At the end of the walk.
Walking time: 1½ hrs.
Grade: Generally easy walking.
Highest point: Starting point Croix de Lognan, 1973m; after that it is only downhill.
Ascent: Hardly worth mentioning; descent

about 700m.
Best time of year: July/August.
Advice: Very unfrequented walk. Shortly before the end of the walk it is possible to go to the south over the Tête des Prapators to Chapeau (see Walk 12) from where there is a splendid view of the end of the Mer de Glace. The detour, which includes a short uphill section, requires 1hr.
Map: ign 3630.

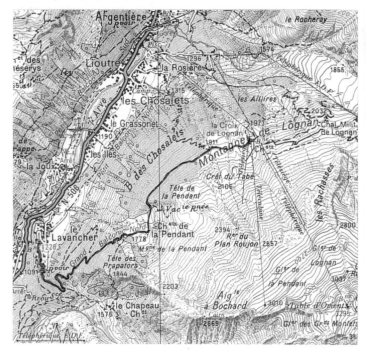

Through the shady forest towards le Lavancher.

Anybody who is sensitive to heat and already knows the south side, i.e. the walks through the Chamonix Aiguilles Rouges, will appreciate the walk from Croix de Lognan to le Lavancher. This route, which is hardly affected by the morning sun, which largely stays lower down, has the disadvantage that the view of the great mountains is sometimes distorted or totally obscured. On the other hand the view of the Aiguilles Rouges is varied and gives the eye a little rest from the exciting contrast of ice and red rock, which is so characteristic of the high mountains.

From **Croix de Lognan** take the path in a westerly direction. It leads past the valley stations of the cable cars and chair lifts, which in summer are rather dreary. After a short descent, enter the woods where at first there is a steep path down to Argentière. Almost immediately you cross the forest and the stream of Pendant, go past the alpine meadow huts of **Pendant** and reach a fork in the path. Now, keeping to the right, go down through the forest, staying right again at another crossing and so reach the path from Chapeau to le Lavancher. Eventually **le Lavancher** is reached by turning off to the right along a road. To return to Argentière it is possible to go almost on the level via the so-called Petit Balcon Nord (about 40 min).

12 Chapeau, 1576m

Walk on the moraine of the Mer de Glace

Les Tines – Chapeau – Les Tines

Location: Les Tines and le Lavancher.
Starting point: Les Tines railway station car park, 1082m.

Food/Accommodation: Destination village.
Walking time: 1½ hrs.
Grade: Generally easy walking. Walking on moraines is often very exposed, as it is here.
Highest point: Chapeau, 1576m: the path can be followed to a somewhat higher point.
Ascent: 500m.
Best time of year: July/August.
Advice: If one starts in le Lavancher the height gain is significantly less: however, one misses out on the impressive view of the glacier stream and the slow unfolding of the details of the Mer de Glace.
Map: ign 3630.

The walk from Les Tines to Chapeau takes a somewhat convoluted route if one wishes to take advantage of as many as possible of the interesting aspects of the walk. At the beginning there is the large glacial stream from the Mer de Glace, then the appearance and increasing proximity of the smoothly scraped cliffs of Chapeau; in the upper part the Mer de Glace itself and the north side of the Aiguille des Grands Charmoz. With a bit of luck to the side of the path on the rocks of Chapeau you will see some climbers on the completely blank-looking slabs. In gazing at the acrobatics it is essential to make sure that one does not dislodge any stones as these could endanger climbers below, who one is not always able to see.

From **Les Tines railway station** go along a path in an easterly direction and then leave this to the right (south) below Côte du Piget. Now go to the south over a small ridge down to a fork in the path on the other side. Further, almost in the opposite direction, follow the path, which goes up along the true right bank of the stream from the Mer de Glace. At a fork, go sharply down to the left, climb up above the wooded ridge and there at another fork, swing back right again in the original direction. Now follow this path upwards in the direction of Chapeau. The direct path from le Lavancher now joins the path. Soon one is above the smooth glacial rocks, which climbers regularly play on in the afternoon. A few minutes later the Chalet at **Chapeau** is reached.

Aiguille du Midi from the track to Chapeau.

The **descent** begins by following the ascent path, but then it takes the fork in the path for le Lavancher in order to provide a more varied overall route. Follow the path into le Lavancher and then turn left down into the woods to finally re-emerge at the railway station of Les Tines. Signpost.

13 Rocher des Mottets

Superb viewpoint below the Drus

Chamonix les Bois – Rocher des Mottets and back

Location: Chamonix, 1040m.
Starting point: Chamonix les Bois car park.
Food/Accommodation: There is no snack bar en route.
Walking time: 2 hrs for the ascent; about 1¼ hrs for the descent.
Grade: Easy walking; path only occasionally steep.
Highest point: 1650m.
Ascent: 600m.
Best time of year: Mid June to mid September.
Advice: From Rocher des Mottets it is possible to follow tracks further upwards in a

southerly direction and reach Montenvers in 1 hr.
Map: ign 3630.

The Rocher des Mottets provides an outstanding viewpoint for seeing the Drus. In particular one can study the Bonatti Pillar at one's leisure. Moreover, the Mer de Glace is also directly opposite and with binoculars you can observe the rock climbers at Chapeau.

From **les Bois** leave the north-eastern boundary road of the village, in an easterly direction until on the bank of the glacial stream from the Mer de Glace, which is not canalised at this point. The so-called Arveyron is crossed by a spectacular bridge which the French call the Pont de l'Himalaya. On the other side follow the path, first to the south, then in a south-westerly direction. At the first opportunity turn off the path to the left and go up relatively steeply through the dense forest (Chemin de la Filia). After a bend at about 1200m take the path in an easterly direction again. After the next bend the wide path is reached, along which skiers normally come from the Aiguilles du Midi to leave the Mer de Glace or the Vallée Blanche. Go upwards along this directly towards the Rocher des Mottets, leaving on the right the path which goes up steeply to Montenvers. After two bends you arrive at the level of the **Rocher des Mottets**.

Descent: If you do not wish to follow the suggestion of continuing directly to Montenvers, whereby you have a pathless ascent of 150 metres of height gain to reach the path to Montenvers, take the ascent path back again. In doing so, it is significantly easier to follow the skiers path via the Chalet de Planards to Biollay, going past the summer toboggan run directly to Chamonix.

The Rocher des Mottets in the centre of the picture below the Dru and Verte.

41

14 Plan de l'Aiguille, 2013m – Montenvers, 1909m

The Henri-Vallot path

From mechanically-assisted means of ascent to mechanically-assisted means of descent

Location: Chamonix, 1040m.
Starting point: Valley station of the Montenvers railway (car park) or car park at the Aig. du Midi cable car.
Food/Accommodation: None en route.
Walking time: 2½ hrs.
Grade: Easy walking.
Highest point: Starting point: 2310m.

Ascent: None worth mentioning.
Best time of year: July/August.
Advice: The more classical route goes via Point 2200m, or the Signal Forbes to Montenvers. This route offers a particularly beautiful view of the Drus and requires an extra hour.
Map: ign 3630.

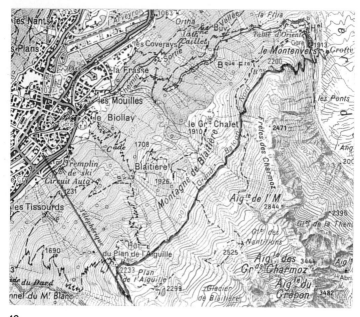

Aig. de Blaitière from the Henry Vallot path.

The Henri-Vallot walk is among the most well known walks in the Mont Blanc Massif. Whoever follows the route in good weather, not in the early morning but in mid morning or better still in the afternoon, will thoroughly appreciate this fact. Immediately below the soaring Chamonix Aiguilles this panoramic path provides ever-changing perspectives of the rock formations. In the morning the path is generally very heavily visited, although the view in the afternoon of the mountains in the western sun is altogether much more attractive. The short cut in the last section of the path, which avoids the ascent to Point 2200, is only to be recommended when you have to hurry; otherwise you are strongly recommended to climb over this little col.

From the **Plan de l'Aiguille cable car station** first of all descend to the so-called **Hotel du Plan de l'Aiguille**. This small hut (30 places) is a bit too near for taking a rest. The path, which takes a generally north-easterly direction descending below the Chamonix Aiguilles, begins here. Almost at the end of it the path splits. Here take the path up steeply to the right via **Point 2200m**, otherwise known as the **Signal Forbes**. On arriving here there is a spectacular view of the Drus and its satellites. The path, which is altogether quite short, allows a visit to the **ice grottos** either via the path, which is well marked, or by taking the cable car.

In **descent** the Montenvers mountain railway is frequently used, although the path down is quite pleasant, as it is not too steep. Here too one should avoid taking short cuts, which not only cause damage to the knees but destroy the forest as well.

43

15 Chalet des Pyramides, 1895m

Panoramic walk over the Glacier des Bossons

Le Mont – Chalet du Glacier des Bossons – Chalet des Pyramides

Location: Chamonix, 1040m.
Starting point: Le Mont above les Bossons or the Chair lift station (car park here).
Food/Accommodation: At the mountain

station of the chair lift, in the Chalet des Pyramides.
Walking time: Without chair lift 2½ hrs; otherwise 1½ hrs.
Grade: Easy walking on mountain slopes which are very steep in parts.
Highest point: 1895m.
Ascent: 850m.
Best time of year: Mid June to mid September.
Advice: From the Chalet du Glacier des Bossons one should not miss the opportunity to take the short path to the ice grotto. It is best to visit the grotto after the ascent to the Chalet des Pyramides.
Map: ign 3631.

The walk over the steep ridge of the Montagne de la Côte to the Chalet des Pyramides is likely to be one of the highlights of a walking holiday in the Mont Blanc Massif. The path zigzags from the steep mountain ridge to the fissured glaciers, rightwards to the Glacier du Taconnaz and leftwards towards the Glacier des Bossons. The latter is the lowest glacier in the Alps, which is surely only indirectly connected with the fact that it lies at the base of the highest summit of the Alps. Due to the reputation of the walk, its easy-to-reach ice grotto and the support from the chair lift, this is a very frequently undertaken walk.

From **le Mont**, a small hamlet above Bossons, follow a minor road, which cuts across the chair lift and which ends in a narrow track. This track leads in many zigzags onto the ridge of the large moraine and then mainly steeply upwards via more bends to the Chalet des Pyramides. The path indeed continues above the **Chalet des Pyramides**, but it becomes more and more difficult and is only to be recommended for experienced mountain walkers. One can, however, go up to the so-called **Gîte à Balmat**, the place where Balmat, one of the first ascensionists of Mont Blanc, spent the night on one of his attempts to climb the mountain. At that time people found it a frightening and eerie place and so it has stayed in the memory.

In **descending** from the Chalet des Pyramides one should not miss out

In the valley.

turning off to the **ice grotto** above the midway station of the Chair lift. To continue down one can take the chair lift, if the car has not been left at Le Mont but rather at the valley station of the chair lift.

16 Grand Balcon (Flegère – Planpraz)

The most famous of all the Chamonix »balcon« walks

Flegère cable car station – Planpraz cable car station

Location: Chamonix, 1040m.
Starting point: Carpark at the cable car station for Flegère – Index.
Food/Accommodation: At start and finish of the walk.
Walking time: 1½ hrs.
Grade: Easy, pleasant walking.
Highest point: About 2000m.
Ascent: Barely 200m.
Best time of year: July/August.
Advice: As the walk is open and south-facing it is often very hot and this must be taken into consideration. If there is no threat of a thunderstorm in the afternoon then it is particularly worthwhile to undertake the walk at this time, as the Chamonix Aiguilles will be bathed in a wonderful light. However, one must bear in mind that it might be necessary to walk back down to the valley if the cable car has stopped running.
Map: ign 3630.

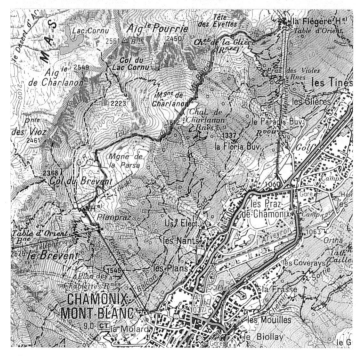

View from Flégère to the Aig. Chardonnet, Argentière and Verte.

The Grand Balcon between Flegère and Planpraz certainly gives the most beautiful walking day in this book for the relaxed walker who shies away from ascents or one who is forced to do so for reasons of ill health. The path from Flegère to Planpraz is almost without uphill sections, has continuously splendid views of the Chamonix Aiguilles and Mont Blanc, and provided it is completely snow-free is absolutely safe. Of course, one is still in the high mountains and the crossing of steep slopes along comfortable paths is part of the normal routine. Due to the great attractiveness of this section of path, one is almost never alone. However, the unique views allow one to tolerate a good deal.

From **les Praz** go up by cable car to **Flegère**. Here the path begins above the hotel and runs in a mostly westerly to south-westerly direction only slightly rising and falling as far as the **Chalet de Planpraz** from where one goes up over a slight ridge and descends in a few minutes to the **intermediate station of the Brévent cable car**. From here glide down comfortably to the valley. If you have left your car at the valley station of the Flegère cable car, then follow the minor road via les Plans and les Nants as far as the N 506. At the level of the les Rosières campsite, cross the valley road and follow the true left bank of the Arve along as far as les Praz. Continue along the bank of the stream to shortly reach the Flegère cable car station.

17 Petit Balcon (Tines – Gaillands)

Small »balcon« offering splendid views and with little ascent

Les Tines – les Gaillands

View from Petit Balcon.

Location: Chamonix, 1040m.
Starting point: Les Tines; best reached by railway; from the end of the walk you can also easily return via public transport. Parking available.
Food/Accommodation: Nothing actually en route, but the path comes close to several places below the route, from where refreshments can be obtained.
Walking time: 3 hrs without hurrying.

Grade: Very easy walking – practically no height gain.
Highest point: About 1200m.
Ascent: About 200m but not very steep.
Best time of year: June – October.
Advice: The walk can be terminated, or started, at various points by walking the 100 – 150 metres from the valley.
Map: ign 3530/3630.

The Petit Balcon Sud, the so-called »small panoramic balcon« leads through the open woods above the floor of the Chamonix valley with little height gain and plenty of views of the mountains opposite. This walk, which can be interrupted at many points, offers a pleasant way of spending an afternoon. It requires practically no fitness and only good

weather. Generally the Petit Balcon is very well sign-posted. Basically the very simple principle is the same as for the Grand Balcon (walk 16): avoid all splits in the path which lead steeply up or down, as the level path is always the right one.

To get to the start of the walk it is best to take the train to **les Tines**. From the railway station cross the N 506 and go through les Tines, crossing the Arve via a bridge and then going into the woods. First up easily following the path,

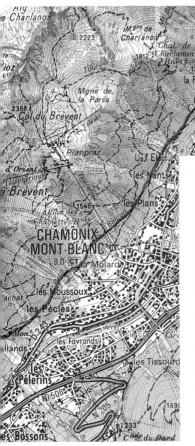

then continue almost always on the level above Praz, Chamonix and les Moussoux, crossing the Brévent cable car line and on past Pelerins and the Lac des Gaillards. Instead of continuing as far as Merlet, go down directly to **les Bossons** where there is a cable car station. If you do continue to Merlet, there is a short uphill section at the very end.

The **descent from Merlet** is either by bus or first along the road and then along a path past the statue of Christ down into the Arve valley basin where a bridge brings one into les Houches. The railway station for the return trip to Chamonix is on the Aiguilles Rouges side!

18 Index, 2385m – Lac Blanc, 2352m

The alpine »balcon« with views

Index cable car station – Lac Blanc – Flegère cable car station

Location: Chamonix, 1040m.
Starting point: Flegère – Index cable car station car park in Chamonix-Praz.
Food/Accommodation: Snack bar at Lac Blanc.
Walking time: 2 hrs without hurrying. Lots of stops needed for viewing.
Grade: Easy mountain walking.
Highest point: Index cable car station, 2385m.
Ascent: Barely 100m.
Best time of year: July/August. It is necessary to make sure that there is not too much snow left: otherwise an ice-axe or trekking poles are to be recommended.

Advice: In good weather there is a high level of exposure to the sun. If one doesn't go down to Flegère or go back to the Index station, but rather walks to Col des Montets it is possible to take the bus back to Praz from there.
Map: ign 3630.

An early morning cable car ascent from Praz de Chamonix via Flegère to the Index takes the mountain walker from the shady valley to the sun-bathed upper terrace of the Chamonix Aiguilles. On leaving the station above on the left is the pyramid of the Aiguilles de l'Index, a very popular destination for climbers. If you then turn towards the sunny side you would have a splendid view of the whole Mont Blanc Massif were it not for the light being against you. Nevertheless, the almost-level walk which now begins offers so many close up objects to view – rock summits, snow fields and numerous climbers pursuing their airy sport – that it is frequently necessary to stop and look. Otherwise Lac Blanc would be reached all too quickly. As

Shortly before Lac Blanc.

with all the walks in the Chamonix Aiguilles Rouges the views of the high rock and ice mountains of the area are best in the afternoon and early evening.

From the **summit station of the Index cable car** follow the path in a north-easterly direction, at first slightly downwards over extensive scree and rock-covered slopes. A short way below a steep rock wall the path bends down to the right (east) and you cross the ridge below the rock face that you have just been admiring. After a further short stretch one arrives at **Lac Blanc**. If it is fairly late in summer, the ice will have thawed and there is perhaps the chance of seeing the Aiguilles Verte mirrored in the surface of the lake.

For the **descent** the rather undistinguished path direct to Flegère is generally taken, although there are any number of other possible descents, whether by going back the same way or by continuing in the direction of Col des Montets or Tré le Champ. (see Walks 8 and 10 in the reverse direction).

19 Lac Cornu, 2276m

Alpine mountain walk to a hidden mountain lake

Planpraz (cable car station) – Col du Lac Cornu – Lac Cornu and back

Location: Chamonix, 1040m.
Starting point: Car park in the valley station of the Brévent cable car.
Food/Accommodation: None en route.
Walking time: About 4 hrs for the round trip.
Grade: Alpine mountain walking on steep slopes, but overall easy.
Highest point: Col du Lac Cornu, 2414m.
Ascent: 550m.
Best time of year: August; earlier in the year there is often snow on the descent from the

Col du Lac Cornu to the lake. It is then best to terminate the walk at the Col, unless one is sufficiently experienced.
Advice: Instead of going back down directly along the ascent path it is possible to descend via the Arête sup. de Charlanon along the Grand Balcon Sud (Walk 16) and to go back to the Planpraz cable car station from there.
Map: ign 3630.

There are not many mountain lakes in the Aiguilles Rouges, nor are these particularly big. Nevertheless, some of them are very attractive due to the impressive mountain backdrop to be found. The Lac Cornu is by no means the easiest of the lakes to get to. The walk over the Col du Lac Cornu onto the west side of the Aiguilles Rouges offers variety on the other side of the crossing, in addition to the well-known view of the many famous peaks.

One can study the sometimes very broken, one can almost say »rotten« rock, from close up. The name of the Aiguille Pourrie, however, has nothing to do with the quality of the rock as might be falsely assumed. Instead this has more to do with the shape of the day's objective, the »horn lake«, even if I personally think that it looks more like an antler. From the **Planpraz station**, 1999m, go up in a north-westerly direction over the rounded hilltop and to the left of the chair lift. This leads to the start of several paths (signposts). First take the path for a short section in the direction of Flegère, until another path goes off from it up to the left. This path rises up gently below the popular rock-climbing peak of the Clocher de Planpraz. After ¾ hr, the path goes up steeply in zig zags to the **Col du Lac Cornu**. On the other side of the Col, the northernmost »horn« of the lake is reached via a large right angle bend. If there is snow, finding the path can be quite difficult here. Moreover, this northern flank has several steep steps and therefore requires particular care.

The **return route** follows the ascent path.

Aig. du Tour and Aig. du Chardonnet with the Lac de Cheserey.

20 Brévent, 2525m

The viewpoint for the north flank of Mont Blanc

Planpraz – Col du Brévent – Brévent and back

Location: Chamonix, 1040m.
Starting point: Car park of the valley station of the Brévent cable car.
Food/Accommodation: At Planpraz (intermediate station) and on the summit of the Brévent.
Walking time: Ascent: 1¾ hrs; Descent: 1 hr.
Grade: Generally easy walking. There may, however, be snow still lying on the north side of the crest of the ridge, which then needs to be crossed with appropriate care.
Highest point: Brévent, 2525m.
Ascent: 550m.
Best time of year: July/August.
Advice: One can take the cable car to the top of the Brévent and walk down. It is, however, more satisfying to walk up, if only to be able to complete one section on foot.
Map: ign 3630.

The Brévent is reckoned to be a particularly worthwhile mountain in this massif in regard to its views. Indeed, the view of the Chamonix Aiguilles on the opposite side, from the Aiguilles du Midi as far as the Grand Charmoz, is exceptionally informative. This is, however, suppressed by the powerful impression made by the giant glaciers which flow down from the summit of Mont Blanc. So one goes up to the Brévent in order to gaze at the glaciers from a safe distance, and with binoculars and a frisson of pleasure to study the route of the Grand Mulets descent from Mont Blanc, which winds its way through the ice falls. However, the view to the north is also worthwhile.

From the **Planpraz Station** cross over a rounded hilltop in a north-westerly direction to the beginning of a number of paths. From here one goes up to the **Col de Brévent**. From the Col itself follow a path on the west side of the ridge: this gradually rises to the **Brévent summit**.

For the **descent** one should not use the cable car, but instead return via the ascent path. The direct path to the intermediate cable car station, which appears to be shorter, lies to the right of this path. At the Col du Brévent keep to the right and the cable car station is reached in just under half an hour.

Path to the Col de Brévent with Mont Blanc in the background.

21 Refuge de Bel Lachat, 2136m

Ridge walk in the Aiguilles Rouges

Brévent – Refuge de Bel Lachat – Merlet – Les Moussoux

Location: Chamonix, 1040m.
Starting point: Valley station of the Brévent cable car (car park); Walk starts on the summit of the Brévent.
Food/Accommodation: Refuge de Bel Lachat.
Walking time: Brévent – hut: 45 min; hut – Merlet: 1 hr; Merlet – valley station of Brévent cable car (les Moussoux): 1 hr.

Grade: Easy downhill mountain walking.
Highest point: Summit of the Brévent, 2525m.
Ascent: Negligible; descent 1450m.
Best time of year: July/August.
Advice: In settled weather this walk is particularly to be recommended in the afternoon.
Map: ign 3530/3630.

Downhill walking has developed a proper tradition, since more and more cable cars have been built in the Alps. There is no room for boredom on this walk, going as it does from the sunny heights of the Brévent to the Refuge Bel Lachat, which offers a rest from the mighty Bossons glacier, then descending further to Merlet on a not very steep path and finally onwards to les Moussoux, the most beautiful place in central Chamonix.

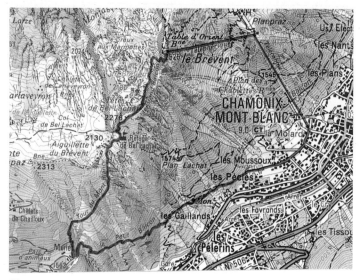

Mont Blanc from the Brévent.

From the **summit of the Brévent,** go towards the path on the west side of the ridge of the Aiguilles Rouge. After a short descent, the path leads almost on the level along the ridge, before arriving at a second step, below which the path splits. After a rest at the nearby **hut** do not take the steep path to the east direct to Moussoux but rather follow the GR5, also at this point followed by the TMB, in a south-westerly direction until you arrive above the houses of **Merlet**. Here leave the GR5 and descend towards the upper end of the road. Now go in an easterly direction via the *Petit Balcon*, slightly descending as far as **les Moussoux** and then along the infrequently used road to the cable car station.

22 Refuge de Tête Rousse, 3167m

High alpine walk at the foot of the Aiguille de Bionnassay

Nid d'Aigle – Refuge de Tête Rousse – Nid d'Aigle

Location: Les Houches or St. Gervais.
Starting point: St. Gervais rack and pinion railway station or the car park of the valley station of the les Houches – Bellevue cable car. The walk begins at the terminus of the rack and pinion railway at Nid d'Aigle, 2372m.
Food/Accommodation: Nid d'Aigle mountain station (not very pleasant). Refuge de Tête de Rousse at the end of the walk.
Walking time: Ascent 3 hrs; Descent 2 hrs.
Grade: A walk which is steep in places and at a considerable altitude. At the end, a flat glacier is crossed. Altogether a high alpine

walk, which is amongst the most difficult in this little book.
Highest point: 3200m.
Ascent: 850m.
Best time of year: End of July and August.
Advice: It is important that not too much old snow is around if the walk is not to be too difficult. The small glacier (Glacier de Tête Rousse) is crossed at the point where it is almost level. It is possible to begin the walk below the Nid d'Aigle. However, it then goes, more or less along the railway tracks, which is not very worthwhile.
Map: ign 3531.

The Aig. de Bionnassay, the local mountain of the Refuge Tête Rouge.

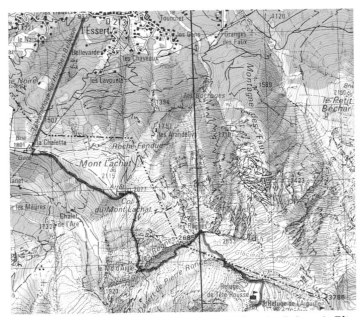

The notable experiences of this walk include a visit to the Refuge de Tête Rousse, situated at almost 3200m, the view of the icefalls of the Glacier de Bionnassay and the endless queue of Mont Blanc aspirants who are here attempting the Route Normal. One is most strongly advised against spending the night at the hut, as the huts on the ascent routes of Mont Blanc are mostly hopelessly overfilled.

From **les Houches** take the cable car to **Bellevue**. Here change to the rack and pinion railway to **Nid d'Aigle**. Here, in addition to the normal ticket, one generally needs a ticket with a number. This shows the number of the train which one is allowed to use. For this reason many passengers prefer to begin in St. Gervais or even in Fayet. On arrival in Nid d'Aigle (»the eagle's nest«) there is no doubt about where the path goes. First go to the northeast, then onto a mountain ridge, always following the large number of other climbers and mountain walkers. Where the ridge becomes almost horizontal there is a small glacier on the right. Here there is a marked track to the **hut**. According to the snow conditions there are various possibilities.

The **descent** is via the ascent route. Glissading down the snow fields to the left of the mountain ridge should be left to experienced mountaineers.

23 Prarion, 1969m

A small summit with a big view

Col de Voza – Hotel Prarion – Prarion – Col de Voza

Location: Les Houches or St. Gervais.
Starting point: Rack and pinion railway station in St. Gervais or the valley station of the les Houches – Bellevue cable car (car park).
Food/Accommodation: Various possibilities. As this path is very much frequented and the ascent is insignificant a pleasant rest on the summit is recommended.
Walking time: Ascent: 1 hr; Descent: ½ hr.
Grade: Easy walking.
Highest point: 1969m.
Ascent: 320m from Col de Voza; if you

return to les Houches by cable car you have to overcome a further 150m to Bellevue.
Best time of year: Mid July to mid September.
Advice: From Prarion it is also possible to descend directly to St. Gervais or les Houches by going in a northerly direction to the Col de la Forclaz, 1533m, and then either left via le Pontet – Montfort to St. Gervais, or to the right via Granges des Chavants down to les Houches.
Map: ign 3531.

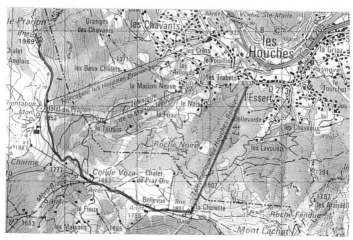

Walks through areas which are used in winter for skiing, are often quite unpleasant on account of the many earth works, which the ski slope builders deemed necessary, and which then remain like wounds in the ground for a very long time. This area too has suffered to some extent from this. Hopefully the short, pleasant ascent, the wonderful view and the enjoyable return path make up for this.

The Aig. de Bionnassay from the slopes of Prarion.

The starting point **Col de Voza** is reached either with the rack and pinion railway direct from St. Gervais or with the les Houches – Bellevue cable car, whereby it is necessary to descend ¼ hr to Col de Voza. From Col de Voza, go up past the lift complex in a northerly direction to the **Hotel Prarion**. Once the buildings are reached, follow the path on the ridge in a northerly direct-ion. After two smaller false summits the actual small **summit** is reached.
The **descent** is normally via the ascent path (see »Advice«).

24 Col de Voza, 1653m

Uphill or downhill walk – according to preference

Les Houches – Col de Voza – Bellevue cable car station – Les Houches

Location: Les Houches.
Starting point: Valley station of Les Houches – Bellevue cable car; parking.
Food/Accommodation: At Col de Voza.
Walking time: Les Houches – Col de Voza: 2 hrs; Col de Voza – Bellevue: ½ hr. If the path is followed in the opposite direction allow 1½ hrs from the Bellevue cable car station to the valley station.
Grade: Easy walking.

Highest point: Bellevue cable car station, 1801m.
Ascent: 800m, or practically none if done in the opposite direction.
Best time of year: Mid June to mid September.
Advice: In an area with as many paths as around the Col de Voza, numerous variations are possible, which can hardly be listed here. These are left to individual creativity.
Map: ign 3531.

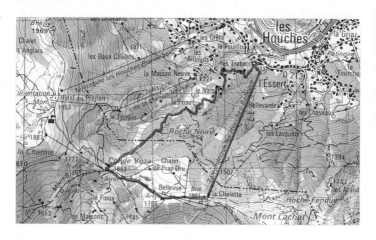

The erstwhile small village of les Houches is nowadays an extensive chalet estate. This is particularly noticeable when ascending from les Houches to Col de Voza. There is a very good view of les Houches, and as one gets higher a fine view of the upper Arve Valley gradually emerges. This is a pleasant walk, which is especially suited to the first days of a mountain holiday as it is partially shaded and the height of Col de Voza, at 1653m, is not noticeable. The walk can, of course, be done in the opposite direction.

Ascent to Col de Voza.

At the **cable car station in les Houches**, a few metres to the west of the station, a minor road begins (marked GR5) which is followed to its end in **Friaz**. From here continue, without any route-finding problems, along the good but sometimes steep path up to the **Col de Voza**. From the Col follow the wide path along the rack and pinion railway in an easterly direction past the **Hotel Bellevue** as far as the **cable car station**.

In **descent** either follow the GR5 (see ascent) as described, or, and this is more pleasant, take the less steep path which begins somewhat to the west of the rack and pinion railway station and descends to the valley and the cable car station via le Terrain.

25 Col de Tricot, 2120m

Round trip via the Col de Tricot

Le Gerdil – Le Champel – Bionnassay – Chalet de l'Arc – Col de Tricot – Chalets de Miage – Maison Neuve – Le Gerdil

Location: St. Gervais or Contamine.
Starting point: Le Gerdil car park. It is also possible to begin from le Champel and to return to there, but it is difficult to drive along the steep and narrow road to Champel.
Food/Accommodation: Bionnassay, Chalet de l'Arc, Chalets de Miage.
Walking time: Gerdil – Col de Tricot 4 hrs; Col de Tricot – Gerdil 2 hrs. The walk is ¾ hr shorter if begun in le Champel.
Grade: Generally easy walking with very steep sections and a traverse below the ice snout of the Glacier de Bionnassay.

Highest point: 2120m.
Ascent: From Gerdil: 1150m. From Champel: 200m less.
Best time of year: August.
Advice: Whoever finds that this route is long should bear in mind that the several kilometre-long rock and ice arête that begins at the Aiguille de Bionnassay - the Tricot Arete, requires a whole day for its ascent. The first ascent of this was among others accomplished by the well-known female German climber, Eleonore Hasenklever in 1905.
Map: ign 3531.

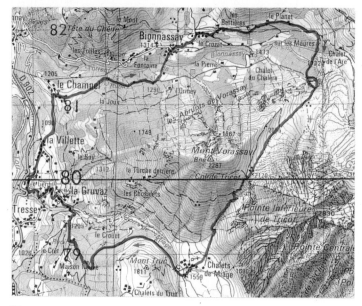

Col de Tricot from the southwest.

This suggestion is a fairly long but extremely varied day's walk. Many different and continually changing impressions can be absorbed. The respectable amount of ascent is best overcome by an early start, especially because in the early morning the long ascent up to the Glacier de Bionnassay is pleasantly in the shade. While descending from the Col de Tricot to the Chalets de Miage, the Dôme de Miage with its towering 2000m high walls is in view.

From **le Gerdil** follow the minor road to **Vilette**. From there take a wide track to **Champel**. Now go up the valley in an easterly direction (waymarked as GR5: TMB) until a fork is reached. Leave the wide track here and go left down to the bottom of the valley crossing over the stream to reach **Bionnassay**. Then follow the road to Crozat and above it take a track in a westerly direction, which leads to the **Chalet de l'Arc**. Now continue below the snout of the Glacier de Bionnassay in a southerly direction upwards to the **Col de Tricot**. After the fairly steep descent to the **Chalet de Miage** cross the stream there and contour on an easy path almost around Mont Truc. At a branch in the path go down to the right via **Maison neuve** in the direction of Gruvaz. From the bridge over the Miage stream there is a path which leads into the gorge, which one can make a note of for a less strenuous day. From **Gruvaz** you unfortunately have to follow the road for a short distance back to **le Gerdil**.

26 Hotel de Trélatête, 1970m

Much visited mountain guesthouse at the foot of the Glacier de Trélatête

Notre Dame de la Gorge – Nant Borrant – Hotel de la Trélatête – Cugnon

Location: Les Contamines, 1167m.
Starting point: Notre Dame de la Gorge. Getting back from Cugnon to the starting point is best done by hitch-hiking or using the infrequent bus service.
Food/Accommodation: Hotel de la Trélatête. Even though it is called a »Hotel« one should only expect the »comfort« of a well-equipped French »Refuge«.
Walking time: Ascent: 2¼ hrs; descent: 1½ hrs.
Grade: Easy walking
Highest point: 1970m, Hotel de la Trélatête.
Ascent: 660m.
Best time of year: July and August.
Advice: From the Hotel de la Trélatête it is possible to reach the Mauvais Pass, via an easterly path which is rather exposed in parts and which ascends about 100 metres. At this point one is at the snout of the Glacier de la Trélatête, access onto which is generally only to be gained with difficulty. If, however, contrary to expectation, it proves relatively easy to get onto at its lower end, it is possible to walk up the scree-covered glacier without worry. Generally, however, the continuation over the northern glacial moraine, which allows access to the Refuge des Conscrits, is more difficult and requires mountaineering equipment, or at least appropriate experience.

Map: ign 3531.

The chapel and the area around Notre Dame de la Gorge are worthy of a day trip on their own. The visit can, however, be combined with the ascent to the Hotel de Trélatête to make a worthwhile, somewhat longer day's work. If, on top of this, providing one has the necessary experience, the detour to the glacier is included, as mentioned above, this really makes the trip into a

View onto the Glacier de Trélatête from above the Hotel de Trélatête.

memorable outing. The walk entices not so much through its distant views but because of the small details on the side of the path: the flowers, the rock formations and the gorge under the glacier.

From **Notre Dame de la Gorge** follow the wide track up the valley in a southerly direction until nearly at **Nant Borrant**. Now go to the left through an open forest on a mountain ridge, over the flank of which the **Hotel de la Trélatête** is soon reached. If you want to walk to the **glacier**, ascend in an easterly direction about a 100 metres in height (signpost: Refuge des Conscrit), before the path winds past steep cliffs to the glacier.

The **descent** from the Hotel Trélatête, can, of course, be made via the ascent path, but it is more interesting to go down via Cugnon, a hamlet on the edge of Contamines. The path begins next to the hotel and goes in a northerly direction. After a few metres it splits. The upper path, known as the *Chemin Claudius Bernard*, is somewhat longer, but more varied. This is followed to a fork in the path, where it is possible to descend to the left in a westerly direction. From the crossroads reached at a forestry hut, it is best to follow the path to **Cugnon,** which provides an only moderately steep descent. From here one can go up to **Notre Dame de la Gorge** along the true right side of the stream (east, good track).

27 Mont Joly, 2525m

Superb viewpoint for the western precipices of Mont Blanc

Le Plan de la Croix (or summit station of the Chattrix chair lift) – Mont Joly and back

Location: Les Contamines, 1167m or St. Gervais, 800m.
Starting point: Le Plan de la Croix or the valley station of the Chattrix chair lift (if in use): carparks.
Food/Accommodation: Pavillon du Mont Joly, 2002m.
Walking time: 4 hrs from Plan de la Croix in ascent; 2 hrs in descent.
Grade: A long walk with several exposed sections. Only for experienced mountain walkers! The walk should only be undertaken in very good weather. In rain or mist, especially in descent, the sloping slate bands are extremely dangerous.
Highest point: Summit, 2525m.

Ascent: 1100m.
Best time of year: August.
Advice: This great walk to a summit with one of the best view points in the whole Mont Blanc Massif can be made into a longer and even more beautiful walk by ascending the Tête de la Combaz from Contamines via Baptien, then crossing over Mont Joly in a northerly direction and returning to Contamines via Moltey, Porcherey, Carteyron and Revenaz. This great mountain walk requires a very early start and would indeed go beyond the boundaries of the recommended walks in this book.
Map: ign 3531.

Mont Joly in the foreground, Dômes de Miage and Trélatête behind.

The view from Mont Joly of the Mont Blanc Massif is of the very highest order. As one is on the crest of the ridge in the main part of the walk, it is essential to stop in order to enjoy the views, as there are places where a stumble could have fatal consequences.

Plan de la Croix is reached on a minor road via St. Nicolas de Véroce. From here onwards follow the wide track, which leads after a bend to a large, wide mountain ridge. This ridge runs parallel to Val Montjoie and the highest point of it is Mont Joly. If the chair lift is operating it is possible to get to this point from Chattrix (recommended). Now go along the east side on a wide slightly rising track until it is possible to go up fairly steeply to the right to reach the height of the ridge. Once on the ridge follow it via **Mont Géroux** (2288m) up to **Mont Joly**. Just below and slightly to the west is found the **Pavillon de Mont Joly**, from where one can obtain both food and lodging.

The **descent** returns via the ascent route.

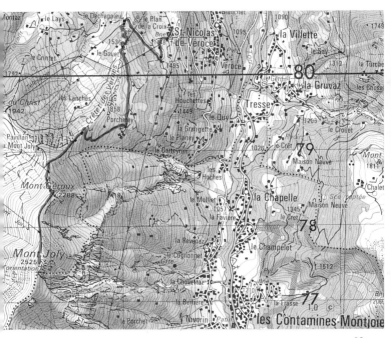

28 Col de la Croix du Bonhomme, 2479m

One of the great sections of the Tour du Mont Blanc

Notre Dame de la Gorge – Chalet Hotel de la Balme – Col du Bonhomme – Col de la Croix du Bonhomme

Location: Chamonix, St. Gervais.
Starting point: Car park at Notre Dame de la Gorge in Val Montjoie, 1210m.
Food/Accommodation: Chalet Hotel Nant Borrant, Chalet Hotel de la Balme, as well as at the start and end of the walk.
Walking time: 5 hrs in ascent; 3 hrs in descent.
Grade: Easy walking, although a rather long ascent.

Highest point: Col de la Croix du Bonhomme, 2479m.
Ascent: 1300m.
Best time of year: Mid July to mid September.
Advice: This long ascent can be broken by spending a night at one of the various »Chalets«.
Map: ign 3531.

Before the TMB gained its present day popularity, this walk in the south-western corner of the Mont Blanc Massif, was a very lonely one. These days in the high season one should expect to come across large groups of walkers. This walk can be done in a day there and back, but this does require considerable stamina, if the real sense of mountain walking – contemplative movement within the natural surroundings of the mountains – is really to

In years with little snow, there is distinctly less snow below the Col de la Croix des Bonhomme than in this picture.

apply. The walk itself sustains interest through the repeated changes in direction, and thus maintains the necessary degree of suspense for the long ascent.

From **Notre Dame de la Gorge** go along the wide valley track in a southerly direction. At first not very steep, shortly below the **Chalet-Hotel de la Balme** the path becomes steeper. Above la Balme the wide track is followed as far as a bend. Just above this the continuation goes off left in a southerly direction. (Shortly after a path goes off left to the Lacs Jovet, also a worthwhile objective for a walk.) Further up the path changes direction again to the south into a narrow little valley, which ends at the **Col du Bonhomme**. From the Col du Bonhomme keep to the left and after only a slight amount of ascent the **Col de la Croix du Bonhomme** is reached, immediately behind which the day's objective is to be found.

The **descent** takes the same route. This path is, however, more to be recommended in ascent with the corresponding continuation along the TMB. Whoever is not stretched enough by the ascent to the hut, can walk on to the Col des Fours, the beginning of the next section (cf. Walk 29). From here it is possible to ascend the nearby Tête Nord des Fours, 2756m. This summit – especially in the afternoon – provides a wonderful view of the Mont-Blanc-Massif.

29 Col des Fours, 2665m

The »summit« of the Tour du Mont Blanc

Refuge du Col de la Croix du Bonhomme – Col des Fours – Ville des Glaciers – Chalet Refuge des Mottets

Starting point: Refuge du Col de la Croix du Bonhomme (see Tour 28).
Food/Accommodation: In Ville des Glaciers.
Walking time: 3 hrs from hut to hut; 4 hrs in the reverse direction.
Grade: No problems as long as the path is free of snow; otherwise an ice axe or trekking poles are recommended.
Highest point: Col des Fours, 2665m.
Ascent: 300m.
Best time of year: Mid July – August.
Advice: In bad weather or when there is a lot of snow, it is better to do walk 30.
Map: ign 3531.

Normally the Col des Fours is the highest point of the Round Walk around Mont Blanc. On account of the proximity of the hut, which is already high up, the ascent is only a short one before the long descent to Ville des Glaciers begins. In order to spare the knees it is best here not to set off too quickly. On finally arriving in Ville des Glaciers the short ascent to the Chalet Refuge des Mottets will be felt as a welcome change. In Ville des Glaciers, the city of glaciers, one might wonder if Tartarin of Tarascon thought up the name, as the only glacier that is visible is relatively modest, but has the prestigious name of Glacier des Glaciers.

From the **Refuge du Col de la Croix du Bonhomme** go back in a northerly direction to the Col itself, then right where the path splits. It is first fairly level then steeper up to **Col du Fours**. From the Col a short detour can be made to **Tête Nord des Fours**, 2756m, (cf. Walk 28). Now it goes down steeply on the east side of the Col. As soon as the ground becomes more level, the path

Waterfall on the descent to Ville des Glaciers.

goes off to the left. After a short, steep step, the path goes over to the left side of the valley. Here various streams have to be crossed, before at **les Tufs**, 1993m, an easy path is reached, which is descended to **Ville des Glaciers**. There is also a steeper, more direct path which can be taken, but which should be avoided as a descent in order to spare the knees. Now continue, as for Walk 30, to **Mottets**.

In the **opposite direction**, i.e. uphill, the walk, quite rightly, is infrequently done. The ascent is completely in the morning sun and offers little in the way of new or interesting views.

30 Chapieux, 1549m

Alternative route with a fine objective for the section

Refuge du Col de la Croix du Bonhomme – Chapieux – Chalet Refuge des Mottets

Starting point: Refuge de la Croix du Bonhomme, 2479m.
Food/Accommodation: In Chapieux.
Walking time: 1½ hrs descent to Chapieux; from there best by bus, otherwise about 2 hrs to the Chalet Refuge des Mottets.
Grade: Easy walk.

Highest point: 2479m.
Ascent: From Chapieux to Mottets: 350m.
Best time of year: July to September.
Advice: This walk is only recommended if it is necessary to go shopping or if the weather is bad.
Map: ign 3531/3532.

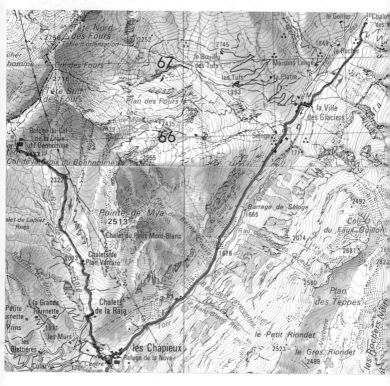

View from Col des Fours in the direction of Albaron.

On the normal route of the TMB the Hut at the Col de la Croix du Bonhomme is the highest overnight stopping point. Consequently one is more likely to be surprised by bad weather or even snowfall in summer here than on the other sections of the route. Then the ascent to Col des Fours (Walk 29) becomes extremely rushed and unpleasant. In such a case the direct descent to Chapieux is inviting. This small village also offers everything normally needed for stocking up on provisions. It is also possible to travel by bus from here to Bourg St. Maurice, if one is fed up with all the walking, the hopefully not really bad weather, or if one simply has a longing for civilisation. As the valley walk from Chapieux to Mottets really does not belong to the best on the TMB, the use of bus or car is recommended. Above Ville des Glaciers there is also a path away from the road.

From the **Refuge du Col de la Croix du Bonhomme** go downwards in an easterly direction, first moderately, then fairly steeply and with many small zigzags. From the alpine meadow huts of **le Raja** it is possible to descend on generally wider tracks, which are easier on the knees. From **Chapieux** to **Ville des Glaciers** the road is the only route. Behind the church in Ville des Glaciers a path turns off right, which leads via a bridge to the other side of the valley. Here continue to the **Chalet Refuge des Mottets**, which is situated on the true left (eastern) side of the valley stream.

31 Col de la Seigne, 2512m

Border crossing to Italy

Chalet Hotel des Mottets – Col de la Seigne – Ref. Elisabetta Soldini

Starting point: Chalet Hotel des Mottets.
Food/Accommodation: None.
Walking time: 3 hrs, of which 2 hrs are uphill.
Grade: Undemanding mountain walking.
Highest point: Col de la Seigne, 2512m.
Ascent: 650m.
Best time of year: July/August.

Advice: The bus stop is about 30 minutes on foot below the Refuge E. Soldini, behind the bridge. From here, in the season, there are buses to Courmayeur. However, it is recommended to continue the round walk via Walk 33.
Map: ign 3531/3631.

In the past, in addition to the Little St. Bernard, the Col de la Seigne offered a not-undisputed border crossing between France and Italy. Today the Col de la Seigne can be crossed without really noticing the border. Smuggling in large rucksacks is also a thing of the past. Changing money is only necess-

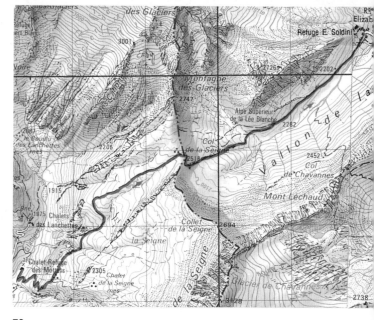

The Col de la Seigne from the west.

ary in order to avoid losing out too much on the exchange rate; and as far as the language is concerned in this part of Italy, French passes perfectly well, if one can speak it. The walk from Mottets is pleasantly uphill in the shade during the morning. When the Col is finally reached, all of a sudden there is a fantastic view of Val Veni and its mountains. Even if they are insignificant in comparison to their surroundings, notice the so-called Pyramides Calcaires on the left, northern edge of the valley. These limestone pyramids seem to have ended up in the wrong place standing here.

From the **Chalet Refuge des Motetts** the track goes up eastwards in zigzags. At a fork, bear to the left (marked) and follow the path in a north-easterly direction fairly straight on through less steep terrain to the **Col de la Seigne**. On the other side it is fairly steep at first, then almost on the level below the Pyramides des Calcaires as far as the **Soldini Hut**.

32 Lac du Miage, 1930m

A gem among the alpine glacial lakes

Val Veni – Lac du Miage

Location: Courmayeur, 1226m.
Starting point: Cantine de la Visaille. It is more convenient to make use of the bus, as the parking places are soon used up.

Food/Accommodation: Below the lake there is a rather uninviting bar! Perhaps this situation will improve in the future.
Walking time: 1½ hrs from the Cantine de la Visaille to the side of the lake.
Grade: Easy, short walk.
Highest point: About 2100m.
Ascent: 420m.
Best time of year: June to September.
Advice: From the side of the lake one should go up the moraine a little on the right (west) side of the Glacier du Miage, in order to better admire the »rocky« glacier.
Map: ign 3631.

The Lac du Miage is unique, even in the Mont-Blanc-Massif where there are so many remarkable natural spectacles. The Italian Glacier du Miage has formed a lake between the moraine ridge and the ice, into which it »calves« at regular intervals. Although it is not possible here to expect a natural spectacle of Arctic dimensions, nevertheless, the ice blocks falling into the calm water create a considerable disturbance in the little lake.

Above the lake, the mighty Aiguille de la Noire towers into the heights and the west face of it can be particularly well appreciated in the early morning when the sun enables its contours to be picked out. The altogether delightful surroundings at the Lac du Miage allow this walk, when combined with a picnic at a suitable point in Val Veni, to become a memorable experience.

From the **Cantine de la Visaille** follow the closed-off road as far as the **Lac de Combal**. Leave the bridge and the road to the Refuge E.Soldini on the left and continue slightly uphill in a semi-circle. Towards the right there are already numerous small paths leading upwards to the lake. These are, however, very steep in parts and therefore unpleasant to walk up. From the building (small snack bar) it is much pleasanter to go up in an easterly direction to the moraine ridge. From here the edge of the **Lac du Miage** is reached immediately.

Lac du Miage with the Aig. Noire.

33 Col Chécroui, 1956m

The large »balkon« above the Val Veni which, quite unjustly, is little known

Ref. E. Soldini – Arp Vielle – Col Chécroui – Courmayeur

Location: Courmayeur, 1226m.
Starting point: Instead of starting as for the circuit from the Ref.E.Soldini (see Walk 31), it is also possible to take the bus from Courmayeur through the Val Veni to Cantine de la Visaille, and to start from there.
Food/Accommodation: Very well-situated snack bar at the Col Chécroui.
Walking time: 3½ hrs. The descent to

Courmayeur is best done by cable car.
Grade: Easy walking; paths seldom steep.
Highest point: About 2350m.
Ascent: 400m.
Best time of year: June to September.
Advice: This walk can be done in various ways, but overall the suggested route appears to be the best one.
Map: ign 3631.

According to the general opinion of those who know the area, this section of the TMB is amongst the finest walks, especially in regard to the views. In places interesting variations can be made on the line of the walk, but here it all depends on finding an easy path, as pleasant as possible and with plenty

of views. In poor weather it is therefore much more advisable to take the bus from Lac Combal and to stroll through Coumayeur, whereby one has to promise oneself to return again when the weather is right. In particular perhaps when in the recent, or more distant past, you have climbed some of the great alpine objectives on the south side of Mont Blanc, it is especially pleasurable to sit in the open under a sunny sky at the Col Chécroui enjoying very Italian food and observing the arena of highly demanding mountaineering with joy and hopefully not nostalgia.

From the **Refuge E. Soldini** first of all go down the poor road to **Lac Combal**. Instead of crossing the stream to the left to the bus stop, go up to the right high above the Alp huts of **Arp Vielle**. Once the next projecting mountain ridge is passed, it is virtually all downhill to the **Col Chécroui**. After a decent rest and as far as possible avoiding looking to the right at the ugliness of the mountain pastures which have been desecrated by the construction of ski slopes, make towards the cable car, with which one can glide back down to Courmayeur. Instead of this, it is also possible to descend the wide footpath via Dolonne to **Courmayeur** (good hour).

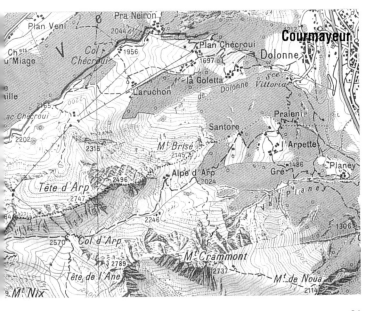

34 Mont Fortin, 2758m

Viewing promontory for the south precipices of Mont Blanc

Lac Combal – Mont Fortin – Lac Combal

Location: Courmayeur, 1226m.
Starting point: Cantine de la Visaille.
Food/Accommodation: None en route.
Walking time: Ascent: 4 hrs; descent: 2 hrs.
Grade: Not so often done in the upper part. Here the path should be as snow-free as possible, otherwise mountaineering experience in crossing steep snowfields is

absolutely necessary.
Highest point: Mont Fortin, 2758m.
Ascent: 1100m.
Best time of year: August.
Advice: On the stage between the Refuge E. Soldini and Col Chécroui (see Walk 33) an ascent of the summit can be included.
Map: ign 3531/3631.

Mont Fortin is the highest of the easily-accessible »viewpoint mountains« on the Italian side of Mont Blanc. Both as an objective in its own right and as a variation on the TMB, Mont Fortin belongs to any demanding walking programme for the area. The view from the summit ranges from the Aiguille des Glaciers in the west, over Trélatête as far as Mont Blanc and its mighty

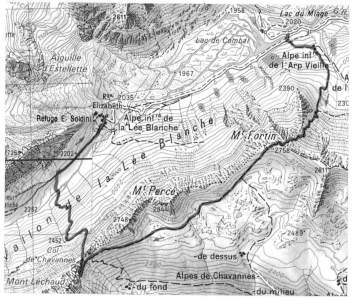

Lac Combal. When there is as much snow as in the picture, the ascent of Mont Fortin should be avoided.

southern precipices. Particularly impressive is the Aiguille Noire de Peuterey. On the summit of Mont Fortin there are still the remains of fortifications. The path to Mont Favre also derives from this period.

From the **Cantine de la Visaille** follow the closed-off road to **Lac Combal**. Cross over the Doire and go up in a southerly direction towards the **Arp Vielle** alpine meadow huts. At the lower hut the path splits. Go right here fairly directly towards **Mont Fortin**. The slope is quite steep, so that if there is still snow here the ascent can be difficult.

Descent: Either go back down the ascent route (care needed on the steep snowfield) or take the almost level path which leads from the summit to the south west to **Col des Chavannes**. From here it is necessary to descend over the north flank, where there is often hard nevé. Go down fairly directly towards the **Refuge E. Soldini**, cross the valley stream and thereby reach the path from Col de la Seigne.

35 Jardin du Miage, 2012m

The Garden in the Glacier

Cantine de la Visaille – Jardin du Miage and back

Location: Courmayeur, 1226m.
Starting point: Cantine de la Visaille. Very limited parking in the main season, so it is perhaps better to take the bus.
Food/Accommodation: Cantine de la Visaille.
Walking time: Depending on one's mood, but at least 1 hr.
Grade: Easy walking. Climbing around in the undulating, slightly overgrown terrain off

the path does demand some sense of direction.
Highest point: Up to about 2000m; usually people only go up to P.1935m.
Ascent: 100 – 300m.
Best time of year: July – September
Advice: There is a certain danger in this area from the streams, which are very fast in places. Caution is absolutely essential.
Map: ign 3631.

The Jardin du Miage is a green island in the middle of the snouts of the Glacier du Miage. A small forest has established itself on the middle moraine of the glacier. One can stroll through the forest, which is predominantly open, and study the whole range of alpine vegetation on the side of the glacier. The best view is obtained by climbing up the northern bank of the glacier. However, the route to the small lake there is somewhat hair-raising, for the icefall of the Glacier du Brouillard is above and occasionally makes itself audible with the sound of falling ice. Another objective is to walk along the glacial stream as far as the snout of the glacier; this section of the walk, without any proper path, is very arduous in parts. Great caution is always required on the side of a glacier where the ice surface steepens. Often there are loose rocks on the surface of the glacier where it becomes flatter, which are not easy to see and which threaten to slide down. In principle one should never go into the snout of a glacier, even if it appears to be quite harmless. A glacial snout is no »show cave«.

From **Cantine de la Visaille** (bus stop) cross the stream above the houses. In general the path leads uphill and down in a north-westerly direction. The second stream, which has to be crossed, can be followed up towards the glacier. In order to reach the little lake, it is necessary to cross a further stream via a narrow bridge. Now continue upwards in a westerly direction. Where the path splits, do not go right in the direction of Ref. Monzino, but left onto the moraine ridge. This is followed to the little **lake**, which lies directly below the high precipices of the lower Brouillard Arete.

Descent: The same way to Cantine de la Visaille. Alternatively, follow the ascent path as far as the narrow bridge. Here, do not cross the bridge, but take the path which forks off in an easterly direction via Freiney and Peuterey to Purtud, where the valley road and the bus stop is reached.

The Jardin du Miage is enclosed by two glacial arms.

36 Mont Chétif, 2343m

Mountain with views above Courmayeur

Le Pra – Mont Chétif – and back

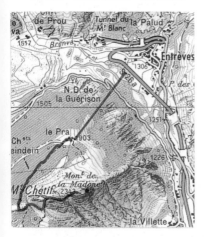

Location: Courmayeur, 1226m.
Starting point: Car park in the valley station of the Val Veni cable car.
Food/Accommodation: The best place is about 20 minutes away in the direction of Col Chécroui.
Walking time: From the cable car summit station: 1½ hrs in ascent; descent: 1 hr.
Grade: Steep in parts and occasionally exposed, but generally easy walking.
Highest point: Mont Chétif, 2343m.
Ascent: 450m.
Best time of year: July to September.
Advice: Unfortunately the surrounding area has been fairly damaged by the numerous roads for constructing cable cars. Whoever is very sensitive to this, would do well to avoid this particular walk.
Map: ign 3631.

The quality of the views from a summit depend very much on the height difference from the objects to be observed. Mont Chétif is a particularly worthwhile example of a viewing promontory. The view from Trélatête in the west to the Grandes Jorasses in the east is a sweeping one. The walk to the summit itself is very short and also very varied. The ascent, assisted by the cable car, leads first of all through an area which has been somewhat damaged by the building of ski slopes. Further on the view opens out onto the actual ski area of Courmayeur, and there one can study very well the unnecessary sins of the piste construction at that time. Unfortunately the attempts at re-grassing the slopes, e.g. on the Brévent, particularly at Planpraz, have not been very effectively begun, so that the ugly view will remain for a good time to come. Nevertheless, the actual objective, the summit of Mont Chétif, the view into the Aosta valley and of the great mountains, is a sufficiently strong attraction for this relatively-short excursion.

From the **cable car summit station at le Pra** on the Val-Veni cable car, follow a road in a south-westerly direction until a small ridge is reached, where a chair lift from the Val Veni terminates. Now continue in an easterly direction, at first without any real ascent. The start of this path is somewhat

Grandes Jorasses from the ascent to Mont Chétif.

difficult to find, the path gets steeper and leads to the level of the ridge. The continuation is through stepped terrain to the **summit**.

In **descent**, if one wishes to avoid the final steep section, it is possible to follow the ridge in a westerly direction (also marked), until this leads steeply down to the left. Even though some roots etc have to be climbed over, this way is better in descent. In ascent the turning off to this route, is however, hardly to be found. From the top of the chair lift go in a north-easterly direction to le Pra.

37 Refuge Bertone, 1991m

Ascent reward with »Aha«-effect

Villair – Refuge Bertone – Planpincieux

Location: Courmayeur, 1226m.
Starting point: Villair, above Courmayeur; no parking in Villair.
Food/Accommodation: Refuge Bertone.
Walking time: 2½ hrs in ascent to the hut. From there via le Pré (20 min) to Planpincieux: 1½ hrs.

Grade: Easy walking.
Highest point: Le Pré, 2125m.
Ascent: 850m.
Best time of year: July to September.
Advice: In order to get directly to Planpincieux, it is necessary to go over the bridge below this small village and then go up again to the right along the road.
Map: ign 3631.

The ascent to the Bertone Hut is certainly not one of the most enjoyable walks in this guide. Also, depending on the weather and wind direction there is the drone of the heavy traffic coming up out of the valley. But as with almost every tribulation, here too there is a reward. As soon as the ridge of Mont de la Saxe is reached, there is suddenly an extensive view, in particular onto the Grandes Jorasses. The continuation of the walk, with a leisurely descent to Planpincieux, brings in addition a wonderful panorama: this is the second, much more gratifying stage of the walk.

From **Courmayeur** go along the road to **Villair** and continue to the end of the road. Now follow the valley path into the Val Sapin. At the fork in the path, which is soon reached, go up to the left in zig zags over a fairly-steep mountain slope to the **Refuge Bertone**. From there follow the ridge of the mountain onto the small summit of **le Pré**. Continue easily in a northerly, then northeasterly direction down to **Leuchey**.

From here a few zigzags lead down to the base of the valley, but it is better to go in a north-easterly direction via **Neyron** down to the valley. Following the valley road downhill, **Planpincieux** is reached in a few minutes. From here return to **Courmayeur** by bus.

Grandes Jorasses from Planpincieux.

38 Col Sapin, 2436m

The great walk through the southern Mont-Blanc Mountains

Villair – Col Sapin – Pas entre deux sauts – Vachey

Location: Courmayeur, 1226m.
Starting point: Villair above Courmayeur; no parking in Villair.
Food/Accommodation: None.
Walking time: 6½ hrs.
Grade: A long and strenuous walk. If after an early start the ascent to the Col Sapin is done in the shade, the rest of the walk is varied and pleasant.
Highest point: Pas entre deux sauts,

2524m.
Ascent: 1350m.
Best time of year: August/September.
Advice: Terminating the walk at the Alpe de Séchéron by a direct descent into the Val Ferret (via Séchéron) would rob the walk of a number of fine views, and is therefore not so recommended.
Map: ign 3631.

Many mountain walkers on the TMB use the bus in the Italian Val Ferret in order to get over this stage of the walk. This is particularly the case because the route over the Col Sapin and the Pas entre deux sauts is little known. This is unfortunate, as from the point of view of the direction of the route, it is a very varied section of the TMB. Here on the south side of Mont Blanc it can get very hot in the middle of summer, which is why an early start is to be recommended.

From **Courmayeur** go to **Villair** and continue to the end of the road. Now follow the valley path into the Val Sapin. Behind the houses of **Chapy** turn off right from the valley path and climb up steeply at first, then more easily, until

behind the houses of **Curru** a steep path leads up over the sun-filled south slope to **Col Sapin**. Now continue in an easterly direction slightly descending to **Alpe de Séchéron**. From here go to the right (SE) as far as a junction, from which the route continues upwards in a northerly direction to **Pas entre deux sauts**. On the other side continue slightly downhill into the Vallon Malatra. Go down through this small valley, always on the true left side (west) of the valley stream. In the lower section descend in steep bends to the valley floor at **la Vachey**.

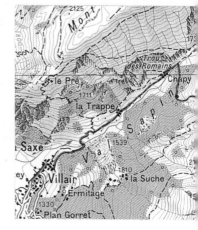

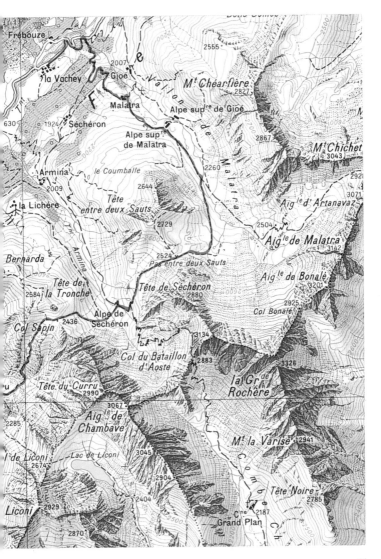

39 Lac Liconi, 2404m

Isolated round walk from Courmayeur

Villair (Courmayeur) – Col de Liconi– Villair (Morgex)

Location: Courmayeur, 1226m.
Starting point: Villair, above Courmayeur; no parking in Villair.
Food/Accommodation: None.
Walking time: Villair – Col de Liconi: 4½ hrs; further to Villair (Morgex): 2½ hrs.
Grade: Strenuous walking away from the popular paths. Descent through the Liconi Valley, which is often very hot.
Highest point: Col de Liconi, 2674m.
Ascent: 1350m.
Best time of year: August/September.
Advice: For the walker who can get up very early it is possible to do this walk in the opposite direction. However, if the Col de

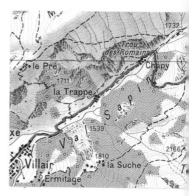

Liconi is reached after 11 o'clock the view of the ice giants of Mont Blanc and the Grandes Jorasses will be strongly impaired by the already high sun.
Map: ign 3631.

The mountains to the south of the great summits of the Mont-Blanc-Massif are not suitable for rock-climbing on account of the friable rock. However, for walking there are many varied routes. The crossing of the Col Liconi, even if it is a fairly lengthy undertaking, is in fact one of the shorter walks. As the sun in this area is a factor to be considered, the impressively deeply cut Liconi Valley is best done in descent.

From **Courmayeur** go along the road to **Villair** and continue to the end of the road. Now go along the valley path into Val Sapin and via the houses of **Chapy** almost into the back of the base of the valley. Here the main track turns off to the right. Follow this almost as far as the houses of **Curru**. Shortly before them a track turns off to the right in a south-easterly direction. It leads up a steep slope to the **Col de Liconi**, which is frequently snow-covered right up to the summer. From the Pass descend in a few minutes to **Lac Liconi**. On the far bank of the lake begins the noticeable, deeply cut and steep Liconi Valley. Particularly in the lower valley the stream has cut deeply into the terrain. Here the path splits. Either – more directly – go right via Planchamp, Fenêtre and Villair to Morgex, or – more easily – via Belle Crête to Villaresson. Now go down along the road in a south-easterly direction, until a path turns off to the west, which leads with only a slight downward gradient crossing the stream from Lac Liconi at the end of the deeply incut gorge. Continue via Villair to **Morgex**.

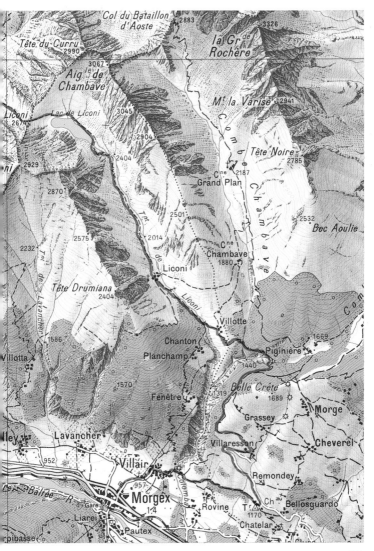

Mont Blanc from the path to Col Chécroui.

40 Vachey – Arnuva

»Balcon« with views above the upper Val Ferret

Vachey – Gioé – Arnuva

Location: Courmayeur, 1226m.
Starting point: La Vachey or the car park somewhat above the second bend.
Food/Accommodation: Arnuva.
Walking time: 2 hrs.
Grade: Easy mountain walking.
Highest point: About 2060m.

Ascent: 400m.
Best time of year: July to September.
Advice: For the return to the starting point at Vachey it is possible in the high season to take a bus from Arnuva.
Map: ign 3631.

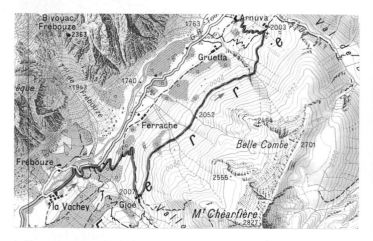

In the main season it can be imagined that the route from Vachey to Arnuva along the valley road is unpleasant. The permanent traffic and the lack of a decent path to the side of the road lead many walkers to use the bus in order to reach the Italian Val Ferret. They, however, miss what is a relatively isolated walking track, which runs along a few hundred metres above the valley. This path, which in parts is hardly trodden and leads along through splendid flower-filled meadows offers a good view into a hardly known corner of the Mont-Blanc area, the mountains around the Glacier de Frébouze. The path itself is almost too short for a half-day walk; if however, one is doing the TMB, this can be combined with Walk 41 over the Grand Col Ferret.

From **Vachey,** go up the valley along the road. After two hairpin bends a fork is reached shortly after a bridge over a small stream at a tiny house. Follow

On the grassy track above the valley floor.

this path, which is very narrow in parts, to the right in numerous zigzags until shortly below the alpine meadow huts of **Gioé**. Now go in a north-easterly direction along a mainly level path which at first is not well defined, and which leads over the most beautiful alpine meadows. The path becomes clearer in the continuation of the walk. After crossing a number of streambeds a further alpine meadow is reached. Here a steep path leads down into the valley with many zigzags, coming out not far from the **Restaurant Arnuva**. From this hotel, which is directed more towards well-off motorists from Upper Italy, it is possible to take the bus to Vachey/down the valley.

41 Grand Col Ferret, 2537m

From the Italian into the Swiss Val Ferret

Arnuva – Grand Col Ferret – Ferret

Mont Blanc from the ascent to the Grand Col Ferret.

Location: Courmayeur, 1226m, la Fouly.
Starting point: Car park at the end of the road to Arnuva.
Food/Accommodation: Fairly near the beginning there is the Refuge Elena; after that there is nowhere else until Ferret.
Walking time: 4 hrs.
Grade: Easy walking on good tracks.
Highest point: Grand Col Ferret, 2537m.

Ascent: 800m.
Best time of year: August.
Advice: In early summer there is often still a lot of snow on the north side of the Grand Col Ferret, but in contrast to the NE side of the Petit Col Ferret this does not necessarily make descending more difficult.
Map: ign 3630/3631.

The crossing from Italy into Switzerland via the Grand Col Ferret is an old connection, similar to that of the Great St. Bernard. Although this connection from Aosta into the Rhône Valley is shorter, the Grand Col Ferret has been spared the pass road, tunnel and exhaust fumes. For a long time walkers have selected this pass as one of their favourite objectives. The change from the sunny, panoramic Italian side to the colder and at first less interesting stretch above Ferret is initially somewhat disappointing. However, on the other hand, new and fascinating sights await the walker. In particular, in the continuation through the Swiss Val Ferret, the warmth of the little hamlets and villages contrasts with those in the two Italian valleys walked through before.

From **Arnuva** go in a north-easterly direction along the wide track towards the end of the valley. At the first of two bends a path goes off left to the Refuge Dalmazzi. Continue along the broad track, which almost resembles a road, as far as a fork. Here go right. Soon after the new Refuge Elena and the Pré de Bar alpine meadow are reached. Shortly beyond the alpine meadow, go right at a fork and now up more steeply along a path which gets narrower, to the **Grand Col Ferret**. On the other side descend easily along a ridge. Then go down more steeply in zigzags to the valley road a short way above **Ferret**.

42 Petit Col Ferret, 2490m

Alpine crossing from la Fouly to Arnuva

La Fouly/Ferret – Petit Col Ferret – Arnuva

Location: La Fouly, Courmayeur, 1226m.
Starting point: La Fouly or Ferret.
Food/Accommodation: Refuge Elena situated on the other side of the Petit Col Ferret, a little above the route.
Walking time: 4½ hrs.
Grade: Difficult mountain walking: on the northeast side there is often névé (hard snow) until late in the year (dangerous!).

Highest point: Petit Col Ferret, 2490m.
Ascent: 900m.
Best time of year: August.
Advice: From the Petit Col Ferret it is possible to make an approximately 1½ hrs detour to the Ref. Biv. du Dolent, a small hut below Mont Dolent and the fissured Glacier de Pré de Bar.
Map: ign 3630/3631.

The ascent of the Petit Col Ferret on the north side leads through a relatively isolated mountain landscape without a particularly spectacular view if one ignores the nearby Glacier du Dolent. Therefore, a detour to the Ref. Biv. du Dolent or a round-trip walk crossing the Tête de Ferret and returning via the Grand Col Ferret, is worth considering. Less recommendable is the crossing from Italy into Switzerland, as the descent of the north side is significantly

Below the Petit Col Ferret.

more unpleasant than it is in ascent, and moreover without the opportunity to pick out the best route in advance.

From **Ferret,** cross the valley stream (Drance) and walk along a path in a northwesterly direction as far as the houses of **Léchère**. Now continue in a generally south-westerly direction along a good track, which follows the stream in a small high valley. Go along the stream past a small lake and keep somewhat to the right to

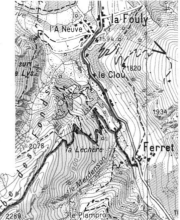

reach the further high valley of the Combe des Fonds. Go up the valley to the **Petit Col Ferret**, which in the upper part mainly involves going up over snow. If you want to traverse over to the **Grand Col Ferret** via the **Tête de Ferret**, 2714m, keep exactly to the ridge. If a detour to the bivouac hut is intended, it is first necessary to descend for several minutes from the Petit Col Ferret before turning off on a track to the right to the hut.

In **descent** to the south the path is fairly rocky and steep down to the alpine meadow huts of **Pré de Bar**. Here one should not miss admiring the curious shape of the Glacier de Pré de Bar. A wide track then leads easily to **Arnuva**.

43 Swiss Val Ferret

A great valley walk

La Fouly – Praz de Fort – Champex

View from the end of the valley into the Swiss Val Ferret.

Location: La Fouly, 1593m.
Starting point: La Fouly car park.
Food/Accommodation: Several huts along the route.
Walking time: 5 hrs.
Grade: Easy, mainly downhill walking, with a rather tough final ascent to Champex.

Highest point: La Fouly, 1593m.
Ascent: 450m.
Best time of year: June to September.
Advice: The valley can, of course, be rushed through by bus, but this walk out from the valley makes a pleasant change.
Map: ign 3630.

The long valley walks are a noticeable feature of the TMB. Generally one is tempted to make use of public transport for such sections. However, the walks through the very different valleys are a considerable attraction of the circuit, whether along the bottom of the valleys or along the »Balcons«. The stretch from la Fouly to Champex has a completely different character to any of the other walks in this book. It goes through a peaceful area, occasionally through a little village, and there is enough time to stop here and there and take some refreshment. It is only at the end that one is threatened by the strenuous ascent to Champex.

In **la Fouly** begin the walk on the left side of the Drance de Ferret at l'A Neuve. The track, which is wide at the beginning, soon splits and you walk up the valley towards Amone. Do not cross the bridge here to the valley road, but continue along the same true left bank of the river. After 2.5km a bridge is reached, above which a snack bar on the valley road can be reached. However, for the continuation of the route, stay on the true left bank. The path splits at various points, but all of the paths on this side of the river

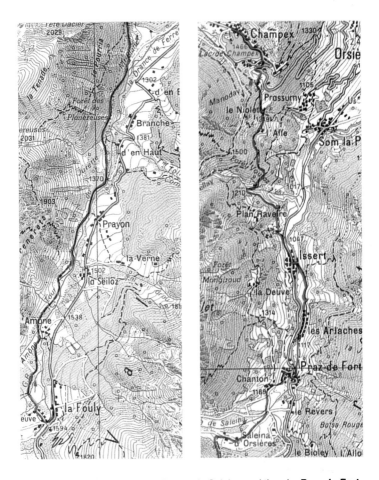

finally reach the bridge over the Reuse de Saleina and thereby **Praz de Fort**. From here go for a short distance along the valley road then right via **Arlaches** to **Issert**. At the end of Issert, turn off left from the valley road. Now follow the slowly rising, well-marked track to **Champex**. This leads right past the swimming pool. After this go round the lake to reach the gîtes d'étape situated on the northwest side.

44 Fenêtre d'Arpette, 2665m

The alpine variation on the TMB through one of the finest high valleys in the area

Champex – Arpette – Fenêtre d'Arpette – Chalet du Glacier – Trient

Location: Champex, 1466m, parking places.

Food/Accommodation: At the beginning at the Arpette alpine meadow.

Walking time: 4 hrs in ascent; 2½ hrs in descent.

Grade: Strenuous mountain walking on tracks which are sometimes steep and exposed.

Highest point: Fenêtre d'Arpette, 2665m.

Ascent: 1200m.

Best time of year: August.

Advice: The walk from Champex to the end of the valley at Val d'Arpette can also be thoroughly recommended for a day's walk.

Map: ign 3630.

The walk through the Arpette valley via the Fenêtre d'Arpette is a worthwhile, if somewhat alpine variation on the main route of the TMB (see Walk 46). From the window there is an impressive view of the Glacier du Trient. The continuation from the window is not at all clear, but the path below steep cliffs is more impressive than difficult. Unfortunately on the descent the view is quickly lost, so that one is pleased to reach Trient, which is more open.

On the ascent to the Col d'Arpette.

From **Champex** the Val d'Arpette is reached via the wide, waymarked track. Continue up along the valley track until practically at the end of the valley the path splits. Now continue to the right in a generally westerly direction directly towards the **Fenêtre d'Arpette**. The fairly steep terrain and the numerous snowfields en route can make progress difficult. From the crossing just below the cliffs go downwards over steep slopes in a generally north-westerly direction. The track improves after the first houses in **Vésevey**, so that the **Chalet du Glacier** is soon reached. From here go either almost horizontally to the **Col de la Forclaz** or over a bridge onto the other side of the valley and along the easy road to **Trient**.

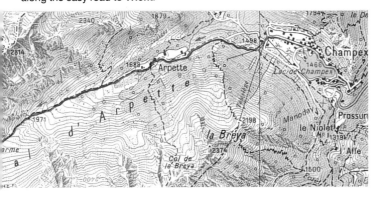

45 Cabane d'Orny, 2811m

Hut walk at the foot of the Glacier d'Orny

Champex (la Breya cable car) – Cabane d'Orny and back

Location: Champex, 1466m.
Starting point: Champex; Cable car valley station car park.
Food/Accommodation: Cabane d'Orny.
Walking time: 2½ hrs in ascent.
Grade: Easy mountain walking.
Highest point: Cabane d'Orny, 2811m.

Ascent: 650m.
Best time of year: July/August.
Advice: Mountain walkers with alpine experience should only go up the apparently easy glacier ascent to the Cabane du Trient with the appropriate equipment.
Map: ign 3630.

The visit to a hut which is used as the starting point for high alpine ascents, is generally found to be something special. This is in part attributable to the atmosphere which emanates from such huts: the different composition of the visitors, the frequent proximity of glaciers and precipices, combined with the

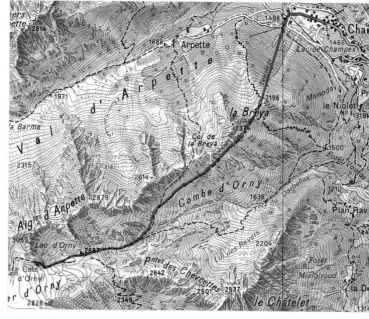

Cabane d'Orny and the north flank of the Portalet.

aura for the walker of the not always easily comprehensible activity of mountaineers. All these factors create a worthwhile objective. The Refuge d'Orny is a beautifully situated goal, which almost perfectly embodies all the above-mentioned characteristics. The hut, first built in the 80s, is just 200 metres higher than the old hut. After the main season one should also consider combining a night at the hut with the romantic experience of a sunset.

From **Champex** first take the cable car to **la Breya**. From here there is a gently upward track in a south-westerly direction, above the Combe d'Orny into the glacial valley of the Glacier d'Orny. The lower of the two lakes is reached, where the old hut stood. From here there is a particularly impressive view of the incredibly steep Tower of the Petit Clocher de Portalet. The **hut** at the upper lake is soon reached via a moraine path.

The **descent** takes the approach route. In doing so keep to the left at the first two forks in the path. At the third fork it is necessary to decide whether to bear right towards the cable car or descend left over the Col de la Breya (almost no ascent) into the Val d'Arpette and from there via the Arpette meadows along the wide track back to Champex.

46 Champex – Forclaz

A day away from the ice and rock giants

Champex – Portalo – Forclaz

Location: Champex, 1466m, very finely situated holiday resort.
Starting point: Champex car park.
Food/Accommodation: None.
Walking time: 5 hrs.
Grade: Long walk without special difficulties.
Highest point: Portalo, 2049m.

Ascent: 750m.
Best time of year: June to September.
Advice: Undoubtedly Walk 44 via the Fenêtre d'Arpette is to be preferred to this walk. However, if the weather is dubious this walk can be entertaining enough.
Map: ign 3630.

In most alpine areas the section of walk from Champex to Col de la Forclaz would count as a walk with many fine views. Here in the Mont-Blanc-Massif, where one is spoilt by the sight of fissured glaciers, huge granite towers and mighty rock faces, this section attracts more through its varied direction.

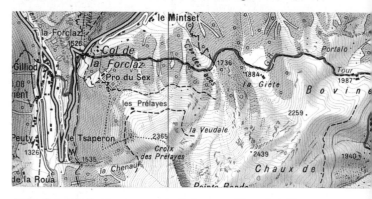

At the Col de la Forclaz an opportunity to ascend in a chair lift opens up an all-inclusive panorama.

From **Champex** first descend via Champex d'en Haut and Champex d'en Bas along a minor road, which mainly leads along the bank of the stream and to the left of the actual road into the Rhone Valley. Below Champex d'en Bas a bridge crosses the stream. After crossing the stream follow the track, which is wide at first, bearing right at a fork in a north-westerly direction. It leads via **Plan de l'Au**, gradually rising in large bends to the highest point of the route, at **Portalo**. The obvious route continues directly to the Col de la Forclaz. To

On the descent from the Fenêtre d'Arpette; the Glacier du Trient on the right.

get from **Col de la Forclaz** to **Trient** take the direct path and not the busy pass road.

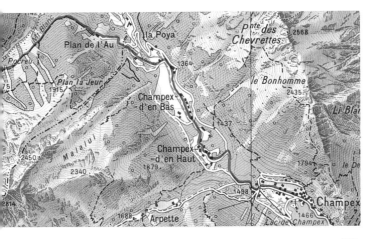

47 Forclaz – Balme

The classic crossing into the Arve Valley

Forclaz/Trient – Col de Balme – Le Tour

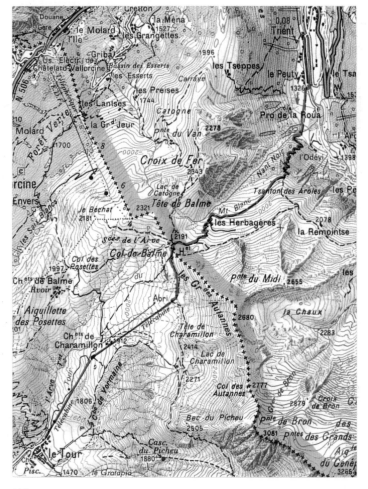

Mont Blanc from le Tour.

Location: Trient, Le Tour.
Starting point: Parking at Forclaz or Trient.
Food/Accommodation: Small hut at Col de Balme, see Walk 1.
Walking time: Forclaz – Trient: ½ hr; Trient – Col de Balme: 3 hrs.
Grade: Easy walking.

Highest point: Col de Balme, 2181m.
Ascent: 900m.
Best time of year: August.
Advice: From Col de la Forclaz a chair lift leads to an especially fine viewpoint.
Map: ign 3630.

In the past the Col de Balme was the logical crossing from the Rhone Valley, once the Col de la Forclaz had been passed. It was only the building of the road that made the stretch via Châtelard and the Col des Montets appear more favourable. Consequently the Col de Balme has been completely left to the mountain walker. On account of its northeast location there is often snow in the gulley on the Col de Balme until the beginning of July: caution is then required. The tremendous view from the pass of Mont Blanc and its satellites is rivetting.

From **Trient,** go along the valley bottom via **Peuty** until the foot of the great gully which comes down from the Col de Balme. On the true right side of the gully (east) the path winds up in continual small zigzags as far as the **Col de Balme**. From Trient there are also other paths via the Chalet du Glacier to the Col de Balme. Although generally longer they are, however, not much more varied.

From the **Col de Balme** either descend to the nearby **intermediate cable car station** and glide back down to the valley or walk back down into the valley.

48 Grand Croisse Baulet, 2236m

The great panoramic summit above Megève

Frasses – Croisses Baulet – Frasses

Location: Megève.
Starting point: Car park at the end of the
road at les Frasses.
Food/Accommodation: None except the
Chalet des Frasses just above the car park.
Walking time: 5 hrs there and back.
Grade: Generally not especially difficult
mountain walking, but as it is partly along the
mountain ridge, it therefore feels a bit
exposed in places.
Highest point: Croisse Baulet, 2236m.
Ascent: 880m.
Best time of year: July/August.
Advice: Strongly exposed to the sun.
Map: ign 3531.

The Croisse Baulet is probably completely unknown to many visitors to
this region, although the summit has
exceptionally good views of the
west flank of Mont Blanc. On first arriving in the Megève Valley the area does
not appear very inviting, but perhaps it is rather friendlier in winter under a
coating of snow. The walk to the Croisse Baulet leads so far away from the
basin of the Megève Valley that it can hardly be noticed. From the summit,
many other walking areas in the region become visible.

From **Megève** drive past the valley station of the Jaillet cable car up a minor
road as far as **les Frasses** (car park). From here first go to the **Chalet des
Frasses**, then on to the top of the ridge. Now go along a track in a westerly
direction to **Col de Jaillet**, 1723m. From here there is a path to the **Petit
Croisse Baulet**. Go down over the rather exposed ridge to the **Col de
l'Avenaz**. The subsequent ascent up to the **Grand Croisse Baulet** follows a
faintly marked track.

The **descent** takes the ascent path. At the Col de Jaillet it is also possible to
turn off right and then follow the first path to the left and so return to the
Chalet des Frasses.

Grand Croisse Baulet.

49 Dent d'Oche, 2221m

The great mountain-walking summit above Lake Geneva

Fétiuère – Chalets d'Oche – Dent d'Oche – Col de Planchamp – Chalets d'Oche – Fétiuère

Location: Evian.
Starting point: La Fétiuère above Bernex and Trossy. Park below the small snack bar, at the beginning of the ascent to the Dent d'Oche.
Food/Accommodation: Hut with guardian just below the summit.
Walking time: To Féutière Hut: 3 hrs; Hut – summit – Col de Planchamp: 1½ hrs; rest of descent: 1 hr.
Grade: The use of a short rope and some basic equipment for protection enables this, the most difficult walk in the book, to be done without problems by children of 10 and

above. The exposed sections on the summit ridge and the protected traverse on the descent can also be avoided by descending to the hut via the ascent route, although this is to be advised against. The basics of mountaineering are essential for this mountain walk.
Highest point: Dent d'Oche, 2221m.
Ascent: 1000m.
Best time of year: July to September.
Advice: As it is on the south side, it is often very hot. The ign map 1:25 000 Morzine 3528 ET is very strongly recommended.
Map: ign 3528.

The Dent d'Oche is situated well away from the Mont-Blanc-Massif. Nevertheless, it is useful to have an interesting day's walk away from the very high mountains. Furthermore, the view from the summit is extraordinarily extensive. Although this is the local mountain for people living on the south side of Lake Geneva, nevertheless, this route presents a challenge for the walker who is familiar with mountains, as there are a number of steep and exposed sections. One part is protected with a chain, which one has to hold onto, or otherwise the climbing is grade II/III. The traverse of the Dent d'Oche suggested here is a very popular walk, and this needs to be born in mind.

From **Evian**, drive via St. Paul-en-Chablais and Bernex to **Trossy**. Just after Trossy at the edge of the forest take a road to the left, which leads to **la Fétiuère**. From here continue on foot along the sign-posted route to the **Chalets d'Oche** (well). Now there is a route which leads through the steep south side of the Dent d'Oche until just below the **Col de Rebollion**. Here climb up a steep gully with rock steps (*some steel cables, beware of loose stones*) as far as the **hut**. From here it is a few minutes along a ridge, which is exposed in parts, to the **summit**.

The descent via this route is not recommended. It is definitely better to descend from the summit via a diagonal line through the steep south flank. Shortly before reaching the Col de Planchamp, a smooth limestone slab has to be crossed (*chain for protection*). After this there is an easy path back to the Chalets d'Oche and to Fétiuère (as for the ascent).

View from the summit of the Dent d'Oche towards the hut and Lake Geneva.

50 Tour du Mont Blanc

One of the most varied walks in the Alps with some of the best views

Rest below Lac Blanc.

Location/Starting point: Chamonix, Courmayeur and many other locations offer themselves as suitable starting points for the Tour of Mont Blanc.

Food/Accommodation: Regularly every 3 to 4 hours.

Walking time: Between 5 and 8 hrs per day.

Grade: This long 7–10 day walk demands a certain amount of stamina and much enjoyment of walking. The best time is the second half of August as the snowfields have generally melted away by then, so that there are no serious difficulties for the walker.

Highest point: Normally not above 2600m.

Ascent: Depending on the route it can vary a lot.

Best time of year: Middle of August to the beginning of September.

Advice: There are many different ways in which the walk can be done. On the recommended maps – ign 1: 25 000, sheets 3531 est and 3630 oest, the line of the TMB is clearly marked. The path too is clearly indicated by good waymarks.

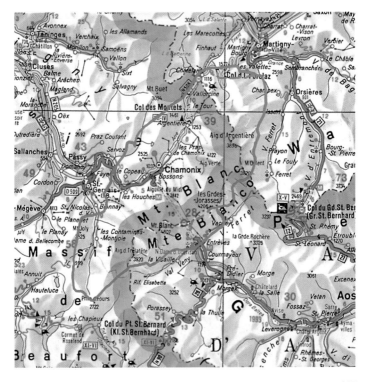

Aiguille de Chardonnet (left) and Aiguille d'Argentière from Flégère.

From the various routes described in this guide, roughly the following sequence should be chosen: 28, 29, 31, 33, 38, 40, 41, 43, 44, 47, 2, 8, 16, 20, 21, 24 and 25. Moreover, there are numerous variations which are described. One of the difficulties which has to be taken into consideration in organising the round walk, is the frequently overfilled accommodation. Therefore it is

recommended for the huts and guesthouses (Gîtes d'étape) to avoid the period from the middle of July to the middle of August. At the beginning of September the holiday season comes to a sudden end in France. Therefore it is necessary to find out if the huts have guardians then, or indeed if they are open at all. However, more and more French people are changing over to the quieter walking season in September for the circuit of Mont Blanc, so that accommodation problems in this period are likely to increase.

Index